DISCOVER · NATURE

around the
House

D1044306

0 11557 03009 9

DISCOVER · NATURE
around the
House

Things to Know and Things to Do

Elizabeth P. Lawlor

with illustrations by Pat Archer

STACKPOLE
BOOKS

Published by
STACKPOLE BOOKS
5067 Ritter Road
Mechanicsburg, PA 17055
www.stackpolebooks.com

Printed in the United States of America

10 9 8 7 6 5 4 3 2 1

First edition

Cover design by Wendy Reynolds

Library of Congress Cataloging-in-Publication Data

Lawlor, Elizabeth P.
    Discover nature around the house : things to know and things to do /
Elizabeth P. Lawlor ; illustrations by Pat Archer.
        p. cm.
    Includes bibliographical references (p.   ).
    ISBN 0-8117-3009-3 (pbk.)
    1. Household animals—Juvenile literature. 2. House plants—Juvenile
literature. I. Title.
QL49.L26 2003
508—dc21

                                            2002156353

CONTENTS

ACKNOWLEDGMENTS

Books of this nature are seldom the work of a single person. I am indebted to many scientists, field researchers, and authors whose work has made this book possible. I am especially grateful, however, to the science specialists who took time from their busy schedules to willingly share their wisdom and knowledge with me. In the course of our conversations, they clarified many points and reconciled conflicting pieces of information sometimes found in the literature. They provided me with valuable reading material in the form of abstracts, papers, and references to important research projects. Some of them took extra time to tell me about their adventures in the field.

The scientists who helped me are Dr. William Stern, Department of Botany, University of Florida, Gainesville; Dr. Alfred Gardner, Curator of Mammals at the National Museum of Natural History, Washington, D.C.; Dr. Natalia Vandenberg, Systematic Entomology Laboratory, Natural History Museum, Washington, D.C.; Dr. Robert Carlson, Systematic Entomology Laboratory, USDA, Beltsville, Maryland; Dr. Robin Moran, Horticulturist, New York Botanical Garden, the Bronx; and Dr. Gary Hevel, Entomology Section, Smithsonian, Washington, D.C.

I also thank Mark Allison, who continues the tradition of excellence at Stackpole Books. His patience, guidance, and editorial skills have helped fine-tune my manuscript.

INTRODUCTION

This book, the ninth in the Discover Nature series, is for people who want to find out about the wild things that thrive in and around their homes. Like the other volumes in the series, this book is concerned with knowing and doing. It is for people who want to get close to nature. It is for the young, for students, for teachers, for parents, for retirees, for all those with a new or renewed interest in the world around us. Getting started as a naturalist requires a friendly, patient guide; this book is intended to be just that. It is intended to gently lead you to the point of knowledge and experience where various field guides will be useful to you. When you have "done" this book, I hope that you will feel in touch with the plants and creatures that live in and around your home.

Each chapter introduces you to a common, easily found living thing that resides close to you and summarizes the major points of interest in the scientific research available. You will learn about its unique place in the web of life and the most fascinating aspects of its lifestyle. Each chapter also suggests activities—things you can do to discover for yourself what each creature or plant looks like, where it lives, and how it survives.

In the first part of each chapter, you will find the important facts about a particular living thing, including some amazing discoveries that scientists have made. You will learn the common names of plants and animals, as well as their scientific names, which are usually Latin. In the second part of each chapter, called "The World of . . ." you will be guided through a series of observational and exploratory activities. This hands-on involvement with plants and animals is certainly the most important of all learning experiences. This is how you will really discover what life in and around your house is all about, something that no amount of reading can do for you.

HOW TO USE THIS BOOK

Feel free to start reading at any point in this book. If you're really interested in daddy longlegs, for instance, and have a chance to observe them somewhere, read that chapter. Then read "What You Will Need" below and "The World of . . ." section of the chapter. This section also tells you what specific science skills are used in the activity. I strongly suggest that you keep a field notebook.

My great hope is that this book will be only a beginning for you. I have suggested other reading to help you learn more than this book can provide. In a sense, when you begin your explorations, you will go beyond all books. Once you get started, Nature herself will be your guide.

WHAT YOU WILL NEED

To become fully involved in the hands-on activities suggested in this book, you'll need very little equipment. Your basic kit requires only a few essentials, starting with a field notebook. I generally use a spiral-bound, five-by-seven-inch memo book. Throw in several ballpoint pens and some pencils and a flexible ruler. Include a small magnifier or hand lens. Nature centers generally stock good plastic lenses that cost a few dollars. You may want to have a bug box—a small, see-through acrylic box with a magnifier permanently set into the lid. It's handy for examining spiders, beetles, and other small creatures; with it you can capture, hold, and study them without touching or harming them. A penknife and several small sandwich bags are also useful to have on hand.

All the basic kit contents easily fit into a medium-size Ziploc bag, ready to carry in a backpack, bicycle basket, or glove compartment.

Basic Kit:
    field notebook
    ruler
    magnifier or hand lens
    bug box
    penknife
    pens and pencils
    small sandwich bags

You may also want a camera and lenses for taking pictures. A three-ringed notebook is helpful for recording, in expanded form, the information you collect in the field. As you make notes, you'll have an opportunity to reflect on what you saw and think through some of the questions raised during your explorations. Consult your reference books and field guides for additional information.

As you read and investigate, you will come to understand how fragile these communities of living things can be, and you will inevitably encounter the effects of humankind's presence. I hope you will become concerned in specific, practical ways and will seek to help make a difference for the future of the environment. We still have a long way to go.

PART I
The Plants

CHAPTER I

Ferns

A TOUCH OF THE VICTORIAN

Many people admire the ornate architecture and styles of the Victorian era. This style originated in nineteenth-century England during the long reign of Queen Victoria. Today homeowners lovingly restore old Victorian houses or build new ones in the grandiose style of that period. The furnishings of a genuine Victorian home usually included prominently displayed ferns. A Boston fern would be the focal point of a room or foyer, overflowing from a large planter atop an ornate pedestal. Many people still cultivate these graceful plants indoors.

Ferns and their close relatives actually flourished in the steamy forests of the Carboniferous period, about 350 million years ago. Flat, marshy land, vast inland seas, and a stable climate contributed to the success of these early land-dwelling plants. The resulting forests of ferns flourished over a large portion of the earth, including what are now the icy polar regions. The cooling climate that followed the Carboniferous period resulted in the evolution of the ferns we see today, which are adapted to changing sets of environmental conditions. Today there are some twelve thousand fern species, about four hundred of which appear in the United States, and about one hundred of those in the Northeast. Ferns of various shapes live in a diversity of habitats, ranging from tropical rain forests to the arctic tundra. Robust, eighty-foot-tall fern trees thrive in the tropics, and dainty, two-inch leaves of curly grass fern (*Schizaea pusilla*) grow in the acid soils of southern New Jersey bogs. You also can find ferns in such unlikely places as the marshlands of northern Alaska and even Antarctica. However, few grow in arid deserts.

Ferns were the first plants with vascular systems. These systems carry minerals and water to food factories in the leaves and then take manufactured nutrients from the leaves to all parts of the plant. They also provide support so that the plants can stand upright.

Ancient mythology often attributed magical qualities to ferns. People noticed that ferns did not possess obvious structures related to reproduction, such as flowers, fruits, and seeds, but the plants continued to appear year after year. Compared with other plants, the ferns were a strange anomaly.

A rudimentary understanding of how ferns reproduce dates back only three hundred years, to 1669, when spores were discovered. At the time, scientists were unable to make the connection between these tiny structures and fern reproduction. It was not until the mid-eighteenth century that this relationship became clear. However, the scientific explanation itself is quite an intricate tale filled with strange terminology.

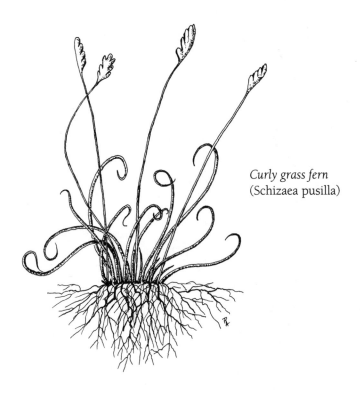

Curly grass fern
(Schizaea pusilla)

Spores are tiny cells that do not contain a baby plant or embryo, and thus do not immediately become new ferns. However, if they fall on suitable soil and have adequate water, they will divide and produce a tiny structure called a prothallium (plural: prothallia). These flat, often heart-shaped structures lack leaves, stems, roots, and vascular systems. They also are very small, growing to about one-fourth inch in diameter, and are only about one cell thick, except near the center. In this slightly thicker region, on the underside, two small structures known as gametes develop. One of these is the archegonium, which contains an egg, and the other is the antheridium, which contains antherozoids, or sperm. Prothallia get their nutrients directly from the surrounding water, which doesn't have to be more than a thin film over the ground. They also need moisture for fertilization to take place, as the antherozoids must swim to the archegonium. The fertilized egg that develops from this union eventually becomes the plant we recognize as the fern. During this development, the prothallium withers, and the young fern becomes self-supporting. Often referred to as the private life of the fern, this first phase in the two-part life cycle of a fern is called the gametophyte generation.

Life cycle of a fern

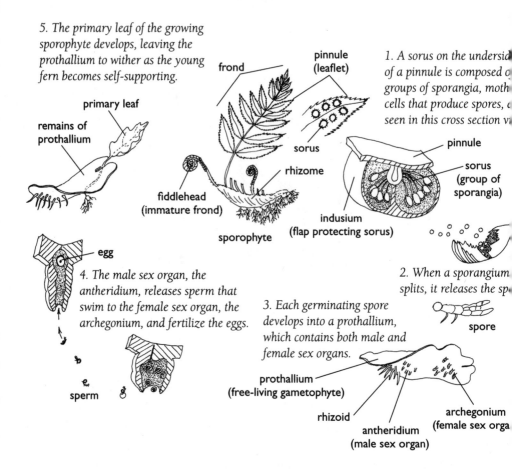

5. The primary leaf of the growing sporophyte develops, leaving the prothallium to wither as the young fern becomes self-supporting.

remains of prothallium

primary leaf

egg

4. The male sex organ, the antheridium, releases sperm that swim to the female sex organ, the archegonium, and fertilize the eggs.

sperm

frond

pinnule (leaflet)

sorus

rhizome

fiddlehead (immature frond)

sporophyte

1. A sorus on the undersid of a pinnule is composed of groups of sporangia, moth cells that produce spores, c seen in this cross section vi

pinnule

sorus (group of sporangia)

indusium (flap protecting sorus)

2. When a sporangium splits, it releases the sp

spore

3. Each germinating spore develops into a prothallium, which contains both male and female sex organs.

prothallium (free-living gametophyte)

rhizoid

antheridium (male sex organ)

archegonium (female sex orga

The self-supporting fernlets have tightly coiled, bright green heads, called crosiers, or fiddleheads, which poke their way through the soil in the spring. As the fern matures, the coils straighten into leaves, or fronds. With the unfurling of its young fronds, the fern enters the second stage of its life cycle, called the sporophyte generation. Now its job is to produce spores. Some ferns produce hundreds of thousands of spores, and other, more prodigious ferns produce millions.

Individual fern species have their own unique patterns of spore reproduction, but generalizations about this process can be made. In the spring, tiny green bumps appear on the undersides of the leaves. As the season progresses toward summer, these bumps turn brown, and the leaves may look as though they are growing fungi. These dark brown spots are called sori, and they contain spore cases, or sporangia. Sometimes the sporangia are covered with a thin protective membrane called an indusium.

When the spores are mature, they are released from the sporangia. The method of release varies among species. In some ferns, the spores are shot into the air by a slingshotlike mechanism. In other species, the sporangia simply open, and the spores are caught in air currents and drift away from the parent fern. Whatever the discharge mechanism, the spores of all ferns become airborne with the slightest breeze, even by an imperceptible movement of air.

Relatively few spores come to rest on suitable soil, but those that land in warm, shady, moist places at the right time of year will begin to grow. If conditions are not appropriate at the time of their landing, the spores remain alive but inactive for as long as a year.

The complete life cycle of a fern is much more complicated than has been outlined here. If you keep in mind the following, however, you can easily remember the essential steps in the cycle: 1. Fronds produce spores. 2. Spores develop into prothallia. 3. Prothallia manufacture gametes. 4. Gametes fuse to produce a new fern. In the activity section, you will have an opportunity to explore this process in some specific ferns.

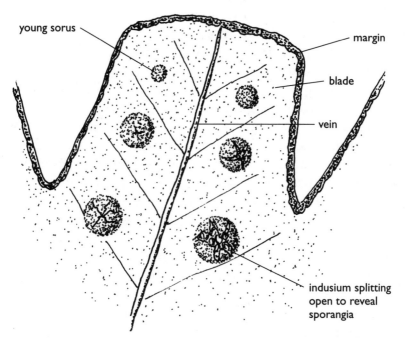

The sori may be scattered evenly over the lower surfaces of fronds or they may be confined to the margins.

This pattern of shifting between asexual (sporophyte generation) and sexual (gametophyte generation) development is known as alternation of generations. Although it is the usual pattern of fern reproduction, not all ferns are restricted to it; some can reproduce vegetatively (without spores or gametes) as well. One way they do this is by the branching and rebranching of their rhizomes (a special type of stem). Some ferns send out a special type of "feeler" rhizome that takes root some distance from the parent fern. When this happens, a new population of ferns appears where there were none before.

Ferns also reproduce asexually by vegetative reproduction of fronds, roots, or rhizomes. This method does not use spores and does not require the union of gametes, and the offspring are identical copies, or clones, of the parent plant. As long as the habitat conditions meet the requirements of the parent plants, the clones and resulting population will survive.

The rare walking fern (*Camptosorus rhizophyllus*) demonstrates another form of vegetative reproduction. Its long, lance-shaped fronds arch away from the center of the plant. When the tips of the fronds touch the earth, they produce roots and new plants, which are clones of their parents.

The Boston fern (*Nephrolepis exaltata bostoniensis*), used frequently as an interior decoration, reproduces vegetatively through the use of runners—stringlike, leafless stems that develop among the fronds. These runners will sprout roots wherever they touch soil.

Buds on the roots of the staghorn fern (*Platycerium* sp.) develop into fernlets. Some less familiar ferns develop clones on the upper surface of their fronds. Eventually the new ferns will leave the parent fern, develop roots and rhizomes, and become independent ferns.

Most ferns are perennials: when it turns cold at the end of the growing season, their fronds turn brown and become brittle. But although their life above ground is over, the rhizomes continue to live throughout the winter. When spring arrives, new shoots will sprout from the rhizomes. If you feel around a clump of ferns in the autumn, you may feel some hard, round forms. These are the beginnings of the fiddleheads that will appear next spring.

Some ferns are evergreen and, along with pines, cedars, and hollies, provide a splash of color to the winter landscape. The common Christmas fern (*Polystichum acrostichoides*), which gets its name from the stocking-shaped lobes of its fronds, is an evergreen fern you might find along wooded, sloping streambanks, near stone walls, and in rocky, wooded areas. The marginal wood fern (*Dryopteris marginalis*) and the rare hairy lipfern (*Cheilanther lanosa*) frequently appear in these environments as well.

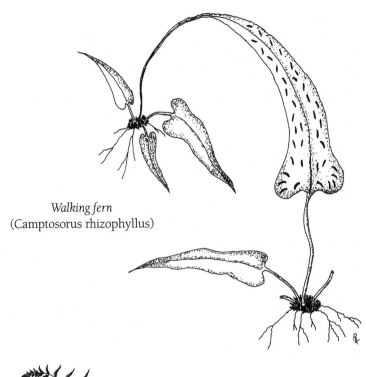

Walking fern
(Camptosorus rhizophyllus)

Marginal wood fern
(Dryopteris marginalis)

Wherever they grow, ferns lend a subtle feeling of wilderness to their habitat. Compared with the cheery spring blooms of wildflowers, ferns are subdued and are easily ignored. However, they can also provide great diversity and beauty. Why not bring some of this woodland beauty into your home? Make a commitment to spend time with these ferns observing them, asking questions, and learning what they have to tell you. Your interactions with them might just develop into a lifelong passion for them.

The activities that follow will give you a new and rich perspective on these fascinating plants that adapt so well to indoor life.

THE WORLD OF FERNS

What you will need	Science skills
basic kit	*observing*
bleach	*comparing*
potting soil	*inferring*
various containers	*recording*
with lids	
gallon jar	
fluorescent bulbs	

OBSERVATIONS

Modern ferns are descendants of the giant ferns that dominated the landscape long ago. Today ferns are smaller and more retiring, preferring to live in nooks and crannies of rocky hillsides or sheltered in the shade along a streambank. People who have grown to love ferns in their natural setting frequently want to cultivate them indoors. How can you replicate the familiar surroundings of ferns in the wild in your home? What kinds of ferns will tolerate the low humidity and high heat of our homes? Can they survive periods of neglect?

Anatomy of a Fern. Ferns lack flowers, fruits, and seeds, which sets them apart from other plants. You can investigate additional characteristics of ferns as outlined below.

Frond, or leaf blade. The flat, green leaf blades, or fronds, the most conspicuous part of the fern, vary in size and shape. Fronds are usually compound, with leaflets attached along a rachis, or midrib. The fronds manufacture food through photosynthesis. The size and shape of fronds vary from species to species.

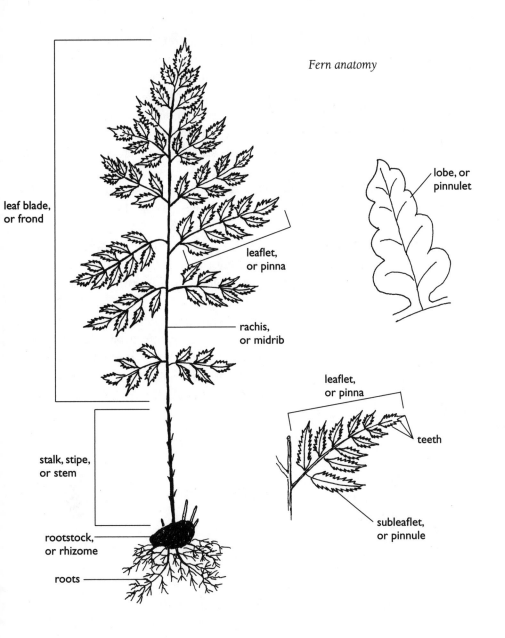

Fern anatomy

leaf blade, or frond

lobe, or pinnulet

leaflet, or pinna

rachis, or midrib

leaflet, or pinna

teeth

stalk, stipe, or stem

subleaflet, or pinnule

rootstock, or rhizome

roots

Leaflet. The leaflets, or pinnae (singular: pinna), are divisions of a compound leaf.

Subleaflet, or pinnule. Subleaflets are subdivisions of leaflets.

Lobe, or pinnulet. Lobes are subdivisions of pinnules.

Teeth. Teeth are serrations along the edges of the pinnae, pinnules, or pinnulets.

Rachis. The rachis is the backbone of the frond and is the continuation of the stalk supporting the leaflets. It resembles the midrib of a simple tree leaf. Until the lobes in a fern are cut to the midrib, there is no rachis.

Stalk. The stalk, or stipe, provides support below the rachis and above the roots. It is covered with hairs or scales, rounded in back and concave or flat in front, and green, brown, tan, silver, or black in color.

Rhizomes, or rootstock. Rhizomes are horizontal stems that lie on the surface of the soil or just below it.

Roots. Roots are thin, threadlike, sometimes wiry structures that anchor the plant and absorb water and minerals from the soil. They grow from the rhizomes.

Fern Identification. You can practice your identification skills by examining the ferns in a nursery or around your house. Look at the shape of the fronds. Are they triangular and broadest at the base, narrow at both ends, or tapered only at the base?

Ferns vary in appearance. Some are extremely delicate; others are more substantial. Lobes, leaflets, and subleaflets can differ from plant to plant. Ferns are organized into groups having similar leaf patterns, which makes fern identification somewhat easier. Botanists who specialize in ferns use an even more detailed system than the one presented here to help them categorize these beauties.

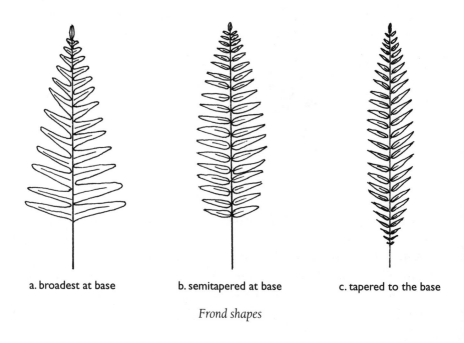

a. broadest at base   b. semitapered at base   c. tapered to the base

Frond shapes

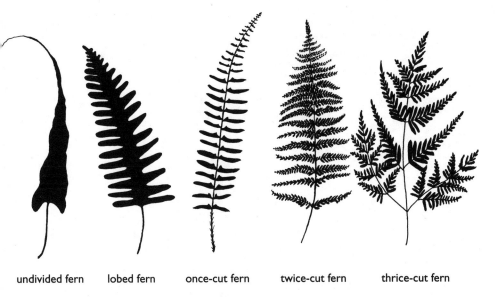

| undivided fern | lobed fern | once-cut fern | twice-cut fern | thrice-cut fern |

Fronds come in many shapes and may be undivided, somewhat divided, or much divided into smaller parts.

Undivided ferns. These ferns are quite different from the typical fern. The simple leaves are straplike and lack the feathery appearance of most ferns. One popular undivided fern is the bird's nest fern (*Asplenium nidus*), a favorite of the indoor gardener. Another atypical fern is the leather leaf fern (*Rumohra adiantiformis*). Its very shiny, leathery, dark green leaves add interest to the indoor garden.

Simple ferns, or lobed ferns. Fronds of these ferns are divided by cuts that lie on either side of—but do not touch—the midrib. The common polypody (*Polypodium virginianum*) has this design.

Compound ferns. The cuts on these ferns extend to the midrib, leaving distinct leaflets. Compound ferns come in the following varieties:

Once-cut ferns. Each leaflet is cut to the midrib. The popular Christmas fern (*Polystichum acrostichoides*) illustrates this cut.

Twice-cut ferns. In these ferns, not only are the fronds cut into leaflets, but the leaflets are also cut into subleaflets. These twice-divided ferns are also called 2-pinnate ferns. Those that can be cultivated indoors include the spider brake (*Pteris multifida Poir.*) and the Cretan brake (*Pteris cretica L.*).

Thrice-cut ferns. In these, the laciest of ferns, the fronds are cut into leaflets, which are cut into subleaflets, which are cut again into lobes. These thrice-divided ferns are also called 3-pinnate ferns. Those that respond well

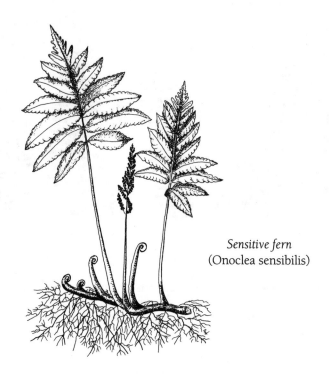

Sensitive fern
(Onoclea sensibilis)

to conditions indoors include rosy maidenhair *(Adiantum hispidulum Sw.)*, dwarf mother fern *(Asplenium daucifolium Lam.)*, and Fiji davallia *(Davallia fejeensis Hook.)*.

Fertile versus Sterile Fronds. Although in many cases the fronds of a single fern will look identical, some species have two different frond types on the same plant. Those that produce spores are called fertile fronds, while those that do not are known as sterile or vegetative fronds.

Fertile fronds often do not resemble the leafy sterile fronds. For example, the shade-loving sensitive fern produces fertile fronds that look like small, thin sticks, each with many branchlets. The sori look like brown beads decorating the tiny branches. These fertile fronds live long after the sterile fronds have withered and died.

Observe the ferns you are growing indoors or those you are cultivating in your yard. Look for signs of fertile fronds. When do the fronds first appear? Do they all appear at once? If not, how long is the delay between frond appearance? When do the sori first appear? Are all the look-alike fronds on your fern fertile or are some sterile? When do the fronds, sterile and fertile, die? On average, what is the lifespan of a frond? How many fronds does one fern produce in a season? Record your findings in your notebook.

Fiddleheads. In the spring, bright green young ferns begin to poke up through the soil. As each emerges, you will see a coil of green called a fiddlehead or crosier. These names refer to the coil's shape, the first for its resemblance to the head of a violin, and the second for its resemblance to the ceremonial staff used by bishops, a stylized shepherd's rod with a crook at the top.

The fiddleheads are coiled because the upper and lower surfaces of the fronds grow at different rates. As the fern grows, the fiddlehead unrolls and expands, revealing tiny new fronds. Sometimes the fiddlehead is covered by fuzzy, brown scales. Certain species of ferns will have a coat of silky hairs on the rachis when the young fiddlehead unrolls. Before the development of synthetic materials, these hairs were taken from large tropical tree ferns and used for upholstery stuffing.

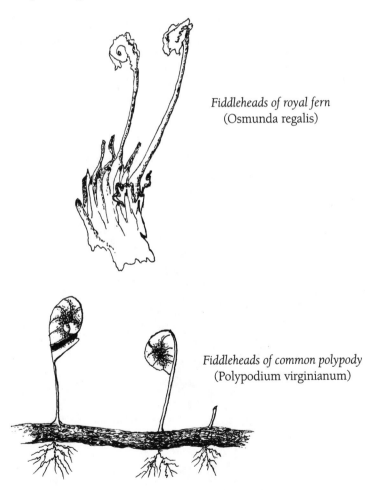

Fiddleheads of royal fern
(Osmunda regalis)

Fiddleheads of common polypody
(Polypodium virginianum)

In the spring, observe either your own ferns or those at a local nursery cultivated for the indoor garden. When does the fiddlehead poke through the soil? Is it wearing a brown, tan, or white fuzzy protective hood? How long does it take to reach its full height? Look for different types of ferns. Do all the ferns you observe have fiddleheads? Which ferns have them and which do not?

In the fall, you can find fiddleheads by poking around the base of the fern. They will be tightly coiled, hard, round structures that hug the rhizomes and may be covered by a thin sheet of soil.

Sori and Spores. Summer is the best time to look for ripe spores. You can tell which spores are ripe by the color of the sori, which will be a shiny dark brown. If the sori are white or green, the spores contained within the sporangia are immature. Withered or torn sori indicate that the spores have been dispersed.

On some ferns, the sori are covered by a thin membrane called an indusium, which can be curved, round, oblong, or narrow. The size, shape, color, and location of the sporangia and indusium vary among species and are used to help identify them.

Cinnamon fern
(Osmunda cinnamonea)

THE PLANTS

Ostrich fern
(Matteucchia struthiopteris)

Bracken fern
(Pteridium aquilinum)

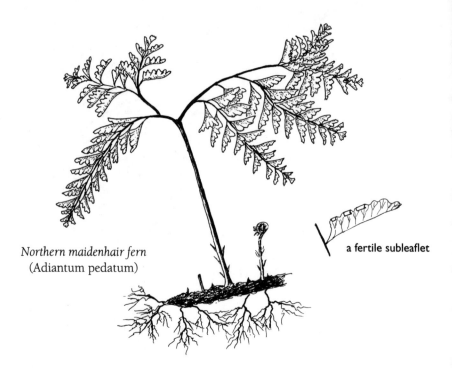

Northern maidenhair fern
(Adiantum pedatum)

a fertile subleaflet

Those ferns that grow well indoors also display sori unique to each of them. The sori on a maidenhair fern (*Andiantum* sp.) are enclosed in the folds along the pinnules. Dense clusters of spores develop on the pinnae near the top of the blade of the Christmas fern (*Polystichum acrostichoides*). The sori of the goldback fern (*Pentagramma triangularis*) develop on fertile fronds and are covered by a yellow powder that gives the species its name.

You can get a good look at spores by removing a mature frond with shiny brown sori and placing it between sheets of white paper. In a day or two, remove the top sheet carefully and pick up the frond. Spores should be present on the bottom sheet.

When did the spores on your fern mature? Are they on all the green leafy fronds or only on some of them? Where on the frond are they located? Are they on a distinctly different fertile frond? Are the sori covered with an indusium? Describe the sporangia. Make a drawing or take a photograph of your fern, perhaps from several different angles. Keep a record of your findings in your notebook.

Stipes. With a knife, cut across the stipes of different types of ferns. Look for the patterns of vascular tubes and compare them on different ferns. Look at those near the base of the stipe and at the top of the stipe. How do they compare? The patterns of the vascular bundles help in identifying fern species.

Growth Patterns. Ferns are perennials. After the growing season, the leaves die, but the rhizomes persist. Each spring, the new fronds grow from one end of the rhizome, while the other end withers and dies. To see the effect of this growth pattern, you will need to mark off the boundary of a clump of ferns during the growing season. Return to that area in the spring. How have the size and shape of the fern patch changed?

Ferns to Cultivate Indoors. One of the first questions posed by anyone who is planning to grow ferns in the house is which plants will do well indoors. On the surface, a fern's needs are simple: light, soil, heat, and moisture. The first three are easy for us to provide, but supplying the proper amount of moisture can be a problem. In the winter our homes are often warm but dry. In fact, we generate a climate that is more suitable to cacti than to ferns.

Ferns that thrive under these conditions are generally those that flourish in the trees of the tropical rain forest, where they grow as epiphytes (plants that grow on other plants without harming the host plant) and require lower humidity than their ground-loving relatives. Those ferns identified below are among those that have good survival records in indoor gardens.

1. Boston fern (*Pellaea rotundifolia*): A trip to any nursery that cultivates ferns is sure to have a supply of these very popular plants for the indoor

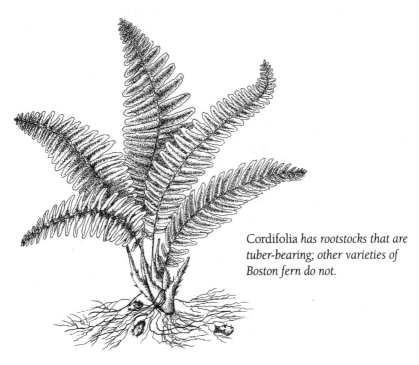

Cordifolia *has rootstocks that are tuber-bearing; other varieties of Boston fern do not.*

garden. They come in a number of varieties. Some have fronds as long as ten feet. Others have an upright growth pattern with feathery fronds.

If you have kept a Boston fern successfully for some time, you will notice brown fronds toward the inner section of the root ball. This is a sign that the fern needs to be transplanted to a larger pot. If this is not practical, you can simply divide the root ball and plant the sections in smaller pots.

Unlike many other ferns, Boston ferns generally do not reproduce by spores. The parent plant will send out long, green, leafless roots called stolons, which turn into tiny fernlets. These can be removed and planted in their own pot.

2. Fuzzy-footed ferns: These ferns are easy to grow. Their exposed rhizomes look like the small paws of a furry animal, an appearance that is actually due to a covering of colored scales. The rhizomes, or "feet," travel over the soil, and if you happen to have the ferns planted in wire containers, the "foot" will push through the openings. New green fronds appear as the "feet" develop. Baskets make ideal planters for these fuzzy-footed ferns. Rabbit's foot (*Davallia* sp.), squirrel's foot (*Humata tyermannii*), and hare's foot ferns (*Phlebodium* sp.) are also good candidates for the indoor garden.

3. Staghorn ferns (*Platycerium* sp.): Staghorn ferns do not display the usual characteristics of ferns. Their large fertile fronds are leathery and resemble antlers, while their sterile fronds cluster together in a shieldlike formation.

Rabbit's foot fern
(Davallia *sp.*)

THE PLANTS

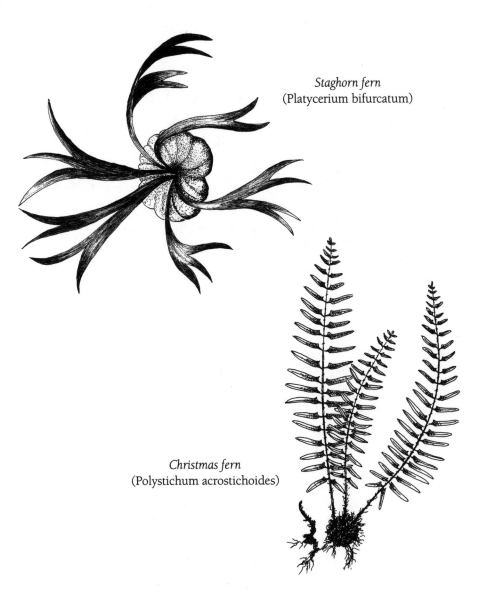

Staghorn fern
(Platycerium bifurcatum)

Christmas fern
(Polystichum acrostichoides)

People who cultivate these ferns often make wall hangings by mounting the "shield" on water-resistant wood. All you need is wall space close to a window.

4. Christmas fern *(Polystichum acrostichoides):* The evergreen Christmas fern is a popular house plant. It produces spores from late summer to early fall on the pinnae of its fertile fronds. Identification of this fern is made easy by the "Christmas stocking" shape of the pinnae. Although this fern is usually seen growing outdoors, it does remarkably well indoors if provided with its essential needs.

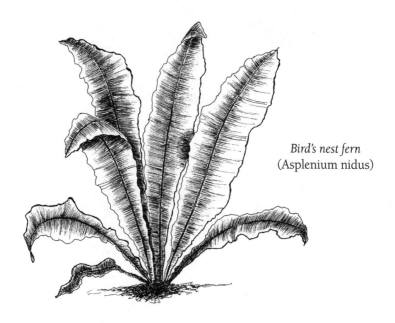

Bird's nest fern
(Asplenium nidus)

5. Button fern *(Pellaea rotundifolia)*: This well-named fern adds variety to an indoor garden. Its leaves reach a length of eight inches, and the button shape of its glossy, dark green leaflets makes it easy to identify.

Popular exotic ferns include:

6. Goldback fern *(Pentagramma triangularis)*: This fern grows well indoors and makes an attractive ground cover when outside. It is sometimes included in rock gardens to add interesting texture. Its tall black stipes add to its interest. Its "semi-marginal" sori are often difficult to find unless you know they are hidden by yellow powder produced by the fertile fronds.

7. Bird's nest fern *(Asplenium nidus)*: Like the staghorn fern, this fern also has leathery fronds, but they are strap-shaped and grow to be about a foot long.

8. Japanese climbing fern *(Lygodium japonicum)*: This is one of several different climbing ferns that do well indoors. This particular fern produces hand-shaped fronds on wiry stems.

EXPLORATIONS

Propagating Ferns. There are several ways you can grow new ferns from old. Fronds, roots, or rhizomes will all develop into a new healthy plant when appropriate conditions are present. Here are two relatively easy approaches to propagation:

1. Footed ferns, those that grow with exposed rhizomes, are easily propagated. All you need to do is cut off pieces of the rhizomes and secure them in the soil with pieces of bent wire. Cover them only halfway with soil.

2. Boston ferns can be propagated from their runners, or stolons, thread-like stems that grow among the fronds and support tiny buds along their length. If you stretch a bud-bearing stolon across some potted soil and clamp it with thin pieces of bent wire, the buds will take root where they touch the soil and produce tiny fernlets. Because the union of gametes (sex cells) is not required in this process, the new fern will be a clone that is identical to the parent fern.

Sowing Spores. Sowing spores is a method for those who are extremely patient and are willing to delay for a long time (several months) their satisfaction in seeing results.

Getting ready. You will need containers with tight-fitting lids. If you lack lids, you can cover an open container with plastic wrap secured with a rubber band. Containers such as these serve two purposes. First, they protect the fern from airborne contaminants such as fungal spores, algae, pollen, and other potentially harmful particles. The tight-fitting lids also keep the system warm and moist, which produces the high humidity necessary for successful germination of the spores.

It is important to emphasize the need for sterile containers and sterile soil. Containers can be sterilized with a 10 percent bleach solution. And instead of using soil, the Brooklyn Botanic Garden suggests a sterile mix of two parts perlite and one part peat moss with time-released fertilizer and micronutrients added. If you are preparing your own soil mix, you will have to sterilize it in a microwave.

Any water you use should be sterilized as well. You can do this by boiling tap water for ten minutes. Distilled water is an acceptable alternative.

You will need a north-facing window to supply light for the container. This will protect the developing spores from the harsh rays of direct sunlight. If you do not have a north-facing window, you can substitute one or more fluorescent light bulbs for this light. The bulbs should be 8 to 20 inches from the incubators, and you should keep the light on for about 14 hours each day.

Be sure to keep the soil at a constant temperature, somewhere between 65 and 75 degrees Fahrenheit. A daily range of about 6 degrees is acceptable.

Collecting spores. Sori that house spores ready to be harvested will be shiny, swollen, and dark brown. If the sori are white or green, the spores inside are too young to produce ferns. If they are torn or tattered, the sori are too old, and the spores that matured there have been dispersed.

Once you have found a frond or pinna containing mature sporangia, place it sori side down on a piece of clean white paper. A paper towel will do nicely and will also absorb water from the pinna, helping to dry it. Cover it with another sheet of clean white paper. Don't forget to put a weighted object on the cover sheet to prevent it from moving. After a day or two, the sporangia will have released the spores, and you will see a collection of tiny, darkly colored particles against the white paper.

While tipping the paper to one side, gently tap it to remove debris such as pieces of dried spore cases. What remains adhered to the paper will be spores. Put the spores in an envelope until you are ready to sow them.

Sowing spores. Sprinkle the spores evenly over the soil and cover the container. In about two weeks (perhaps sooner) you will notice a green film on the soil. This tells you all is going well. The developing threadlike prothallia cannot be seen without a hand lens. In five months' time a mat of prothallia will have formed on the soil. If the container looks crowded, you have too many prothallia; you can thin them by slipping a rounded knife blade under the mat and gently removing fingernail-sized clumps. Experts suggest wiping, with bleach solution, any tool you may use, as well as your fingers.

It may take the prothallia as long as twelve months to produce the sporophyte, but generally you can expect some sign of development after about six months. When the sporophyte does develop, you will probably have to thin the prothallia again. As growth continues, you will see more fronds, and you can remove the covers from the containers.

Indoor Pests. Aphids, scales, spider mites, and mealybugs are the insects that most often plague ferns growing indoors. While there are chemicals you can use to rid your ferns of these pests, you can also achieve desirable results with their natural enemies.

Ladybugs are especially fond of aphids. One ladybug species, the convergent beetle (*Hippodamia convergens*), is an especially good choice for ridding ferns of this pest. Another natural enemy of aphids is the green lacewing, which belongs to the family Chrysopidae. Green lacewings also enjoy a meal of either adult or young scale predators.

Spider mites can be eliminated by adding predatory mites, which are smaller than their prey. These tiny arachnids will devour both adult spider mites and their eggs.

An effective way to control mealybugs is by introducing tiny beetles called crypts (*Cryptolaemus* sp.).

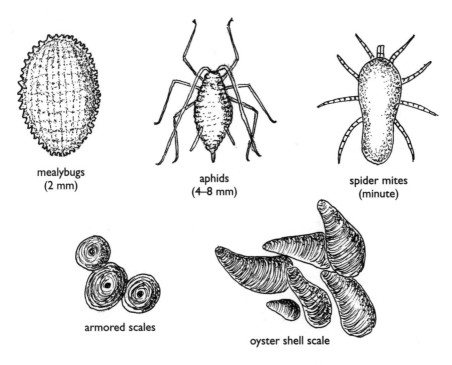

mealybugs
(2 mm)

aphids
(4–8 mm)

spider mites
(minute)

armored scales

oyster shell scale

Common Indoor Plant Pests (not to scale)

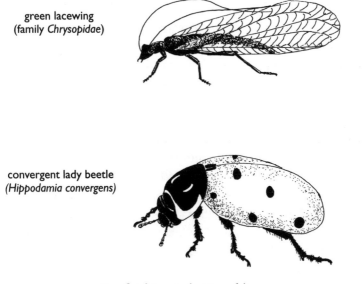

green lacewing
(family *Chrysopidae*)

convergent lady beetle
(*Hippodamia convergens*)

Beneficial Insects (not to scale)

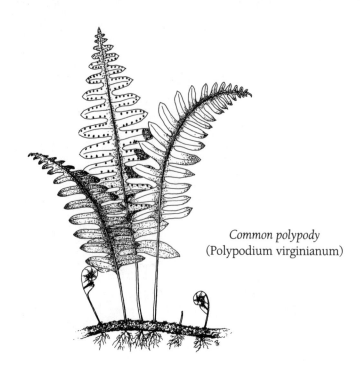

Common polypody
(Polypodium virginianum)

Creating a Terrarium. A terrarium is a tiny greenhouse that will allow you to enjoy ferns throughout the year. To create one, you will need some simple and easily obtained materials.

First, wash a wide-mouthed gallon jar thoroughly with very hot water, then wash it again and allow it to dry. For drainage, line the bottom of the jar with a layer of gravel or small chunks of clay from broken pots to a depth of about one inch. Add about one-quarter inch of charcoal—this will absorb the gases that decaying vegetation in the soil will produce. At a nursery or supermarket, purchase a small bag of sterile potting soil, and add it to the jar to a depth of about two inches. The soil needs to be light and airy (potting soil usually contains loam for this purpose).

Ferns best suited for a terrarium are small and slow-growing, such as the fragile fern *(Cystopteris fragilis)* and common polypody *(Polypodium virginianum)*.

The plants in the terrarium need water, light, and air. How to supply these needs and to what extent they should be supplied will vary according to your particular circumstances. The following suggestions are based on those in *Ferns and Their Allies,* by Edward Frankel.

Light. Put your terrarium near a window where it will receive northern light—direct rays from the sun will prove deadly. You can also use artificial light, as described in the "Sowing Spores" section. Experiment to find out what conditions are best for your ferns.

Water. The amount of water needed will vary depending on the size of the terrarium, where it is located, and the type of ferns planted. You do not want the soil too wet or too dry. If the ferns look healthy, you are probably providing the right amount of water.

Air. As the plants need some air, only partially cover the top of the wide-mouthed jar with a small plate made of glass or plastic.

How to Learn More. One of the best ways to learn about ferns is to join a group of like-minded people. To find out about groups near your home, write to The American Fern Society, Department of Botany, Milwaukee Public Museum, 800 W. Wells St., Milwaukee, WI 53233, or call the New York Botanical Garden, (718) 817-8700.

CHAPTER 2

Cacti

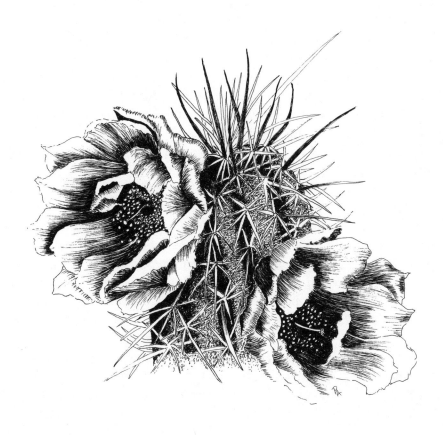

DESERT DENIZENS

Arid, hostile, hot, punishing, and downright unpleasant are some of the descriptions often applied to deserts. Many people consider deserts to be places of dull, muted colors with short, shrubby plants and scrawny trees that don't offer much protection from the searing heat of the midday sun—sandy places where a variety of prickly cacti are always ready to stab the careless visitor. The few mammals and reptiles unfortunate enough to live there, they believe, spend their time hidden beneath rocks or in underground hideaways.

Often these opinions belong to those who have never been to a desert. Their knowledge frequently comes from movies, TV shows, or novels, which have given them a distorted view of desert life. Others have based their beliefs about deserts and desert life on nothing but a short drive through desert terrain on their way to somewhere else. Perhaps they saw only an occasional bird fly across the path of their car. Or maybe they learned about other life forms by sighting a lizard posed on a roadside rock. Even the dictionary describes the desert as "a region so arid it supports only sparse and widely spaced vegetation or no vegetation at all." All this adds up to the overall impression that life in the desert is difficult, if not downright cruel.

No one mentions the transformation that occurs in desert life after a seasonal downpour. Then the landscape bursts into a colorful tapestry of plant life. In the infrequent springtime rain, short-lived wildflowers spread their palette across the desert floor. But it is the cacti, in all their splendor, that are significant contributors to the exquisite, breathtaking hues. The desert afternoon has become a floral wonderland. Some cactus blooms are strikingly colorful, while others are more subdued. Some open during daylight hours; others confine their display to the dark of night.

Although the vast majority of cacti are native to North America, the land now covered by desert in the western United States (see Chapter Note 1) did not always support this ecosystem. About 100 million years ago, most of the land was covered by water, and the rest was a steamy hothouse in which tropical plants flourished. Warm winds from the Pacific Ocean carried moisture-laden clouds over the region and supplied it with an abundance of life-sustaining water. It was there that the ancestors of today's cacti developed and thrived.

Geological evidence tells us that about 60 million years ago, those conditions began to change as the result of some earth-shaking events. The earth's crust was slowly thrust upward, and mountains were formed to the west of this inland sea. This change had a significant impact on the animal and plant life of the region. Clouds that once supplied moisture were forced up the new

THE PLANTS

coastal mountain slopes. This caused the air in them to cool, and they dropped their moisture on the western side of the mountains. Cooled, dry air then descended the eastern slopes. The wind still blew from west to east, but now it was hot, dry air that evaporated the inland sea. What had once been a tropical greenhouse dried up and became the deserts we know today.

Rainfall in these deserts does not exceed more than ten inches per year, but there are deserts in the world that receive even less than that scant amount. Death Valley within the Mojave Desert of the United States receives only two inches per year.

The rare desert rainfall can trigger a series of dramatic events. In New Mexico's desert, for example, torrential downpours frequently produce extremely dangerous flash floods. The water from these rains drains into dry channels called arroyos. These savage, rushing waters have been known to destroy everything in their path, including cars and people. As soon as the sun returns, the water collected in gullies quickly dries. If you are spending time traveling in desert regions, obtain accurate, up-to-date weather reports so that you can avoid these life-threatening events.

Before the inland seas dried out, conditions favored plants with green leaves and stems. As the landscape began to dry out, conditions for living things began to change as well. To survive, plants had to adapt to the changing environment. Among the plants that survived those geological upheavals were the ancestors of present-day cacti. This makes cacti some of the newest plants on earth. To put this into context, the first land plants began evolving about 400 million years ago; the ancestors of today's flowering plants showed up about 130 million years ago; and cacti appeared only 40 million years ago.

In the early days of this struggle, one survivor was a spiny evergreen with thick, waxy leaves and thick, woody stems with green bark. The root system of this plant was designed to rapidly soak up all the water within its reach, and its bark manufactured food. The descendants of this early survivor are alive today. They are the members of a genus called *Pereskia*. Unlike the typical cactus, members of this group of cacti have broad, green leaves, which they keep throughout their lives. Another noncactus quality is the tropical woodland habitat in which *Pereskias* grow. Scientists believe these plants are the descendants of the first cacti that appeared following the massive geological reorganization. Today some *Pereskias* resemble bushes, while others are climbing vines. They can be found in Florida, the Caribbean, and southeastern South America. Some varieties are suitable for hanging plants on a porch or inside your home.

From this beginning, more and varied cacti developed that differed considerably from the green plants that flourished in the early tropical environment. To understand how cacti function in today's deserts, it is necessary to examine some of their survival strategies.

In an ecosystem where water is scarce and disappears quickly after it falls, cacti have developed efficient, widely spreading root systems. This allows them to absorb water quickly from a large area. The roots of a large saguaro cactus reach out about fifty feet, forming an underground circle that lies close to the surface. This is important, since rainfalls in the desert are generally brief, and water can pass quickly through the soil.

Cacti also have evolved an interesting strategy for storing water. Their fleshy stems, which put them in the category of succulents (see Chapter Note 2), are filled with spongy cells that can hold large amounts of water. As a cactus absorbs the water through its root system, its spongy interior stores the

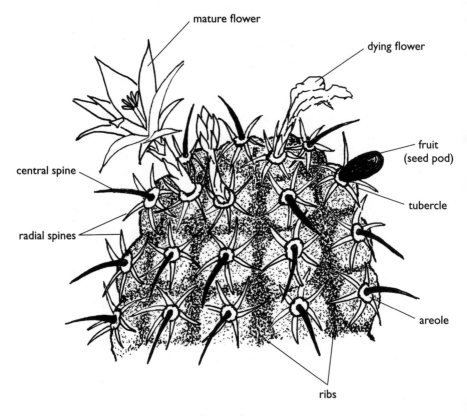

Generic Cactus

water and swells. The reserves, stored in the cells, are used by the cactus during the long periods of drought that follow desert rains. A giant saguaro may store as much as four or five tons of water in the spongy pulp. To support this heavy weight, the towering saguaro has an internal support system of woody ribs that functions as an internal skeleton.

Even the smallest cactus, sold in local supermarkets, has a series of vertical, accordionlike pleats. When a cactus has soaked up water and is filled or nearly so, the pleats are not very distinct. As the cactus uses up the stored water, the pleats become more obvious. Thus the interior volume of the plant can increase without any increase in surface area . . . very clever!

Excessive loss of valuable water would be tragic for any plant. To avoid this disaster, cacti have developed several interesting adaptations. With the exception of the *Pereskias,* cacti are leafless. Green leaves are essential for the survival of most plants. They have large surface areas for capturing the energy in sunlight, which they use to manufacture nutrients. Each leaf is a miniature factory powered by the sun. The large surface area of a leaf has another function: It contains openings that conduct water vapor out of the plant. Cacti carry on these functions without leaves by capturing sunlight and manufacturing nutrients within their green stems. As done in the leaves of other green plants, water is transferred from the roots to food factories in the leaves where, together with carbon dioxide from the atmosphere, it is used to produce nutrients. Excess water from this process is transpired as vapor from the cacti through relatively few tiny, widely spaced pores, or stomata, in the stems. In leafy plants, the stomata are greater in number and in size and are mostly located in the leaves.

The skin of a cactus has a waxy quality, similar to that of a cucumber. This waxy substance on the skin, known as a cuticle, helps prevent water loss.

Spines are additional water-saving devices. They come in a variety of sizes, shapes, and colors. Desert winds can be very strong. The spines minimize the drying effects of wind by deflecting it away from the cactus. They also reduce the force and speed of the wind, which in turn reduces the amount of moisture that it can remove from the cactus plant. This is another clever solution to the problem of living in a dry, windy environment.

Some cacti are endowed with hair in addition to spines. The golden old-man cactus (*Cephalocereus chrysacanthus*), which has gray or white hairs so long and thick that they nearly cover the spines, uses another moisture-saving strategy. The hairs function in much the same way as the spines do in protecting the plant from water loss, by countering the drying effects of the sun and wind. Mammal hair and bird feathers provide similar protection.

When there is a good water supply, green leaves make it possible for leafy plants to manufacture food quickly. Because of the short supply of water, cacti cannot afford to be fast food factories. Therefore, their growth rate compared with that of leafy plants is very slow. It takes six years for a saguaro to grow six inches, and in twenty-five years it will have reached only three feet.

In the desert, large cacti grow in isolation from other plants. They are surrounded only by sandy soil and perhaps some stones and rocks. This is especially true of the large saguaro and other big cacti. Spacing such as this is the result of their far-reaching root systems. If other cacti were too close, they would endanger themselves, as well as their close neighbors. Prickly pear and cholla are exceptions to this survival strategy.

Besides the members of the cactus family, many other types of plants and a variety of animals, including kangaroo rats, lizards, sidewinder snakes, and big-eared foxes, make their homes in the desert. Cacti are nourishing food sources, and most desert animals eat their stems or other parts. Piglike animals called javelinas or peccaries depend on cactus pads and fruits for food and moisture. Prickly pears and chollas make up a significant portion of their diet. In total, about forty kinds of animals, including deer, pronghorn antelope, and cattle, rely on prickly pears for nourishment. Some rodents chomp on fleshy bulbs and tubers, and the scattered seeds are eagerly picked up by ground squirrels, among others. The Harris ground squirrel depends on prickly pears for about two-thirds of its food and drink. Hordes of insects dine on desert plants, including cacti. Bats wing their way through the desert by night, feeding on these insects. You can see that the cactus is an essential element at the base of the desert food chain.

Giant saguaro cacti also provide homes for many birds. Gila woodpeckers peck nest holes in the stems. Elf owls move into these holes when abandoned by the woodpeckers. Harris's hawks make their nests cradled in the crooks of inviting saguaro branches.

Survival is a difficult challenge in the desert environment, and only the well-adapted survive. What is surprising is that there are so many plants, insects, and other animals that have adapted, met the challenges, and thrive in what appears to be a barren wasteland.

Caution: When working with cacti, wear heavy gloves to protect your hands.

OBSERVATIONS

Cacti belong to a group of plants called succulents, which means juicy or full of water. The ability to store water in their leaves or stems is a trait that separates succulents from other plant groups. Cacti have certain characteristics that set them apart from other succulents such as agave, sedum, and aloe. For example, most cacti do not have leaves. They store water in their green stems, which are also their food factories. The notorious spines of the cactus grow out of areoles, white cushions that look like tiny patches of cotton on the stems. Although many other succulents have spines, only in cacti do they grow from areoles. Cacti are also unique in that they originated only in the Americas.

Cacti make great house and patio plants for those whose thumbs are only a faint shade of green. They require little watering and scant fertilization, and, in fact, they thrive on a little neglect. Their beautiful blooms, intriguing spines, and long lives reward you for not fussing with them. In addition, the warm temperatures and dry air in many homes provide ideal conditions for these desert-loving plants. And don't worry about being bored with only a few choices; there are thousands of different kinds of cacti.

To help you become acquainted with cacti in the following activities, you will need to have a few different kinds. Don't take them from the wild; buy them from legitimate growers or visit a nursery or greenhouse that specializes in these fascinating survivors (see Chapter Note 3).

The Anatomy of a Cactus

Spines. The first thing that may strike you as you observe a cactus plant is its spines. As you examine different cacti, you will notice that the spines come in a variety of shapes, sizes, patterns, and colors. Many devotees raise cacti as much for the decorative qualities of the spines as they do for the flowers. The illustrations represent some of the various types of spines. (*Note:* In some species, the spines of the mature cactus differ from those of a young plant. This difference often makes identification difficult.)

Shape. Spines come in the following varieties:

• Ascending. The hedgehog cactus has an upward-curving central spine surrounded by radial spines.

• Hooked. *Mammillaria* sp., such as the fishhook pincushion, and *Ferocactus* sp. cacti have hooked central spines.

• Sheathed or covered. The touch-me-not teddy bear *(Opuntia bigelovii)* has sheathed or covered spines.

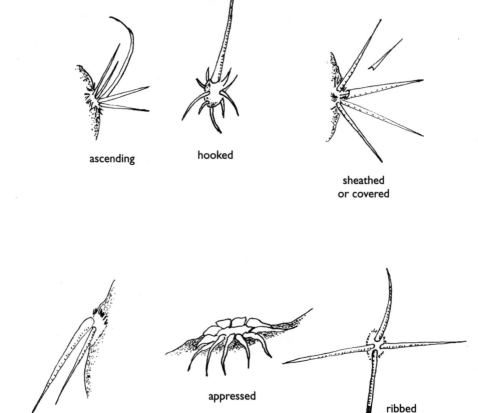

Examples of Cactus Spines

- Deflexed. Strawberry hedgehog cacti (*Echinocereus engelmannii*) have deflexed spines.
- Appressed. In the lace cactus (*Echinocereus caespitosus*), the spines form a comblike pattern and lie flat against the stem.
- Ribbed. The tubby touch-me-not (*Ferocactus wislizeni*) has long, strongly ribbed central spines. The longest is hooked.

Examine the spines of several different species of cactus plants. How many different kinds of spines can you detect? Are all the spines on a cactus plant similar, or do you see more than one type on a cactus? For example, is the center spine downcurved and the surrounding spines straight? Do the spines grow singly or in clusters? Make drawings of the different kinds of cacti and their spines.

Look carefully at the place where a cluster of spines is attached to a cactus stem. You will notice a small, fuzzy cushion of white material. This is called an areole, which comes from a Latin word meaning "small area." A hand lens will give you a better look. How would you describe the cushion? Make a drawing of a spine cluster. Don't forget to include the areole.

Roses and blackberries are known for their thorns. You might suppose that spines and thorns would be closely related plant structures. They are not. The thorns of these plants are modified branches, whereas the spines of a cactus are modified leaves. Examine a few thorns and compare them with the spines of a cactus. Draw a picture of thorns on a rose or blackberry stem. Do the thorns grow singly, or in clusters like the spines of cacti?

Color. Cactus spines come in a range of colors. The radial spines of the fishhook barrel cactus (*Ferocactus acanthodes*) are gray, but the four central spines are red. Other cacti have white spines, and the spines of still others are yellow and various hues of red-orange. You can expect to find gray and black spines as well. Some spines look as though the tips were dipped in paint.

Find as many different cacti as you can to determine the variety of colors present in the spines. In your sample, are all the spines on a particular cactus the same color? How many different colors did you find? What color was the most common? What do you think the advantage is for the cactus to have white or light-colored spines (see Chapter Note 4)?

Glochids. These are sharp, barbed hairs that grow out of the areoles. They may look like innocent tiny hairs, but if you touch one, you will find that they penetrate your skin and are extremely difficult to remove. Unfortunately for us, these barbed bristles grow on those cacti that are most often cultivated indoors. Prickly pears (*Opuntia* sp.) have these tiny hairs growing out of the areoles either in addition to spines or in place of them. If you have

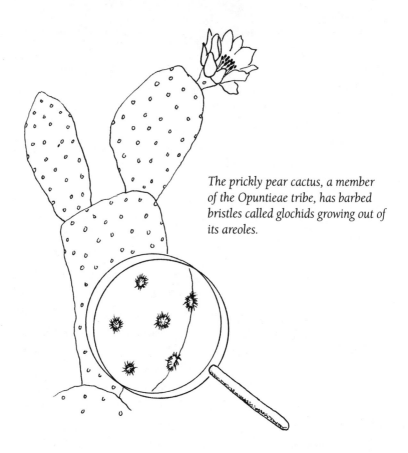

The prickly pear cactus, a member of the Opuntieae tribe, has barbed bristles called glochids growing out of its areoles.

an *Opuntia* be extremely careful, and keep a pair of tweezers handy. The bristles are difficult to remove, and the wounded area will remain painful even after they are removed.

Flowers. Cacti produce exquisite flowers, which is another reason why people cultivate them. Cactus flowers may be funnel-shaped or wheel-like. How would you describe the shapes of the flowers on your cacti?

Flower orientation. When your cacti are in bloom, you will see that the flowers grow from the areoles. The flowers on different types of cacti do not grow from the same place on the stem. The location of the flower is an important characteristic used in identifying cacti. Flowers appear in the following spots:

• Off the side of the stem, as in peanut cactus (*Chamaecereus silvestrii*) and hedgehogs (*Echinocereus* sp.).

• Forming a ring at the top, as in old lady cactus (*Mammillaria hahniana*).

• Singly on the top, as in bishop's cap (*Astrophytum myriostigma*).

• Two or more at the top, as in silver ball cactus (*Notocactus scopa*).

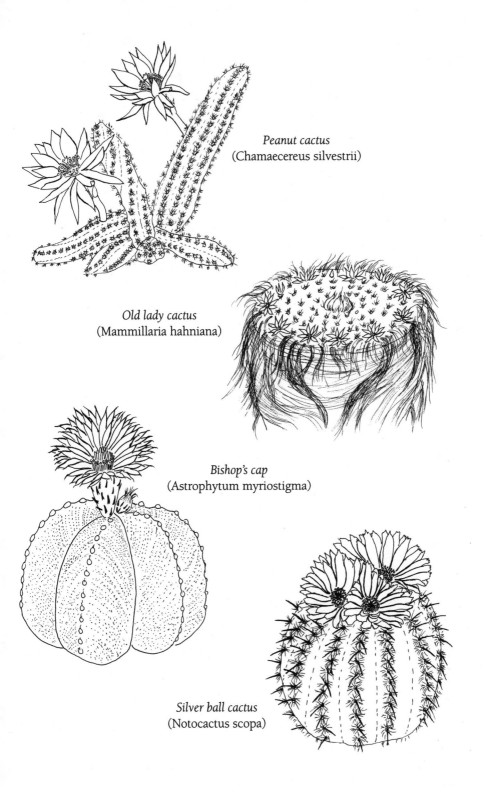

Peanut cactus
(Chamaecereus silvestrii)

Old lady cactus
(Mammillaria hahniana)

Bishop's cap
(Astrophytum myriostigma)

Silver ball cactus
(Notocactus scopa)

CACTI   **43**

Parts. Although flowers have a variety of shapes, they all share some basic features. There are four parts to the flowers of almost all flowering plants: sepals, petals, stamens, and pistils. Unlike many other flowers, those of the cacti have numerous stamens, petals, and sepals.

• *Sepals.* The outer leaves of the flower. Their job is to protect the flower when it is a bud. Usually they are green, but they may be the same color as the colorful inner leaves, or *petals.*

• *Stamen.* The male part of the flower. It is made up of the anther, which produces pollen, and a filament, a thin, stemlike support for the anther. Cactus flowers have many stamens.

• *Pistil.* The female part of the flower, made up of the stigma, style, and ovary. The stigma is the sticky, pollen-receiving part of the pistil, which is elevated by a slender style and connects with the ovary at the base of the pistil.

• *Ovary.* In most flowers, the ovary is above the petals and sepals. In cacti, however, the ovary is below those parts.

Cactus Tribes. When you start studying cacti, you will soon discover that there is a confusing collection of these plants. It is helpful to divide the cacti into three groups, which botanists call tribes. These groups represent the progress cacti have made along the evolutionary trail, from their primitive forms to the more advanced forms that are more familiar to us. The following

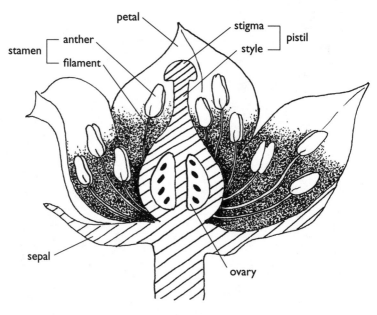

Parts of a typical flower

THE PLANTS

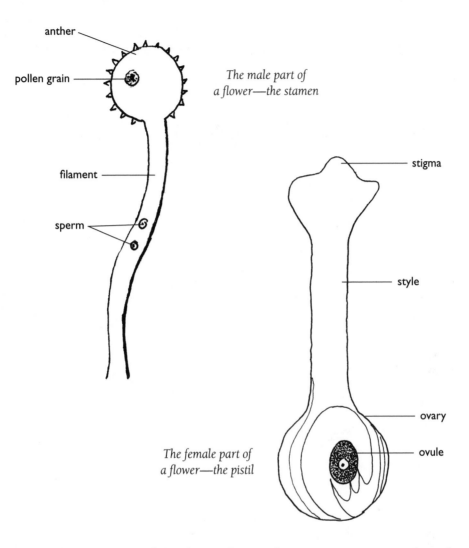

anther

pollen grain

*The male part of
a flower—the stamen*

filament

sperm

stigma

style

ovary

ovule

*The female part of
a flower—the pistil*

are brief descriptions of the three tribes, with a representative member of each that you could cultivate indoors.

Pereskieae tribe. The cacti in this group are the most primitive, or the last connection between the cacti we know today and other leafy plants. They are native to the generally dry tropical forests. Physical characteristics that identify them are broad, succulent leaves, a sprawling growth pattern, and woody stems that are succulent inside. Their spines, stems, and wheel-shaped flowers grow from areoles. *Pereskias* are similar to their evolutionary ancestors in that they have leaves that produce food as well as food-producing stems. There is only one genus present (*Pereskia* sp.), which makes this group the smallest cactus tribe.

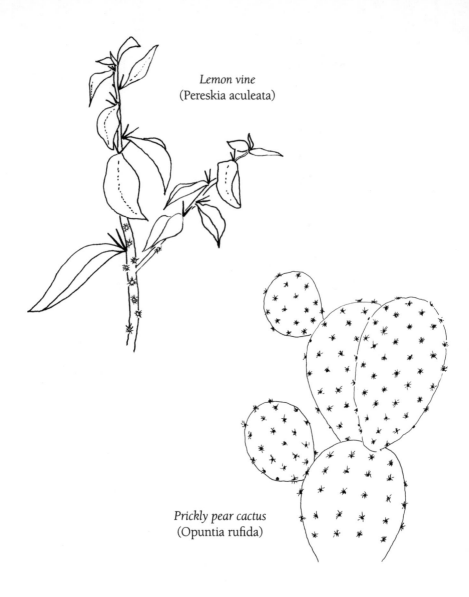

Lemon vine
(Pereskia aculeata)

Prickly pear cactus
(Opuntia rufida)

Lemon vine *(Pereskia aculeata)* makes a good hanging plant. Be careful of the spines hidden under the lemon-scented leaves. Unfortunately, the yellow flowers generally don't appear in cultivated plants. In its natural setting, the red fruits that appear after the flowers die back are known as Barbados gooseberries.

Opuntieae tribe. Opuntias are also like their evolutionary ancestors in that they have leaves for a brief time in their early development. They are the most common of the cacti, and members of this tribe are the cacti most often cultivated by indoor gardeners. Opuntias (botanists pronounce every letter) are the only cactus to have glochids. These tufts of barbed bristles are the hallmark of this group, and they can cause pain if the unwary should get pierced by them. The water-retaining pads serve the same function as stems in other types of cacti and are unique to this group, even though not all Opuntias produce them. Chollas are an example of padless Opuntias.

The sausagelike stems of teddy bear cholla (*Opuntia bigelovii*), the pads of bunny ears (*Opuntia microdasys*), and the flat pads of other *Opuntia* sp. have taken over the food-making function of the leaves present in the Pereskieae tribe. All but two genera of the Opuntieae tribe have glochids and spines. The grizzly bear prickly pear sports prickly spines, and the worrisome beaver's tail (*Opuntia basilaris*) is spineless, with reddish glochids growing out of the aeroles.

Most Opuntias have tiny leaves on new stems. These leaves fall off when the stems mature.

The flattish, wheel-shaped flowers that appear on the stems are a hallmark of these cacti and separate them from the Cereeae tribe below. Some of the Opuntias have large, juicy fruits, and the fruits of some desert-growing prickly pears are sold in supermarkets.

Cereeae tribe. Members of this large tribe occupy the highest rung on the evolutionary ladder. The group holds about 75 percent of all cacti. Botanists have separated the tribe into eight subtribes. These subtribes have characteristics that identify them as members of the tribe Cereeae but that distinguish them as belonging to a specific subgroup. The Cereeae may have only one stem or may be many-stemmed. None of them has glochids, but a few have a hair or two at each areole. All have funnel-shaped flowers. To further confuse the beginner, individual members vary greatly in appearance from one another. Some are giant cylinders, others are tiny globes, and still others are flat-stemmed. They thrive in a variety of habitats, from moist, tropical jungles to dry deserts.

Cereus subtribe. Most of these cacti are very spiny. The flowers appear along the sides of the stem. The slow growth of the *Carnegiea gigantea,* a saguaro in this subtribe, makes it a good houseplant. Although it grows to twenty-five to sixty feet tall in its natural setting, it takes about ten years to grow only six inches. This cactus is of interest to the indoor gardener, as it has two distinctly different kinds of spines. Those near the bottom of the plant are gray and may be straight or curved, while the spines above these are straight and yellow.

Another cactus in this subtribe of interest to the indoor gardener is *Stenocereus thurberi,* the organ-pipe cactus. In the wild, this cactus can reach twenty feet, but because of its slow growth rate, it can make a handsome addition to an indoor collection.

Hylocereainae subtribe. One of the most spectacular members of this subtribe is the night-blooming cereus *(Selenicereus grandiflorus).* Its ribbed gray-green to purple stems can grow to sixteen feet in length, but it can be trained to climb an indoor trellis. The long, tubular flowers appear along the side of the stem. The petals are pure white inside, with a touch of salmon on the tips. These nocturnal flowers have a powerful fragrance, often said to have a touch of vanilla. Many indoor gardeners invite friends to witness the blooming of these wonderful flowers, which last only a few hours.

Echinocereinae subtribe. *Echinocereus* is one of the largest groups in this subtribe. They are very spiny, and the stems have ribs. Plants are globe-shaped

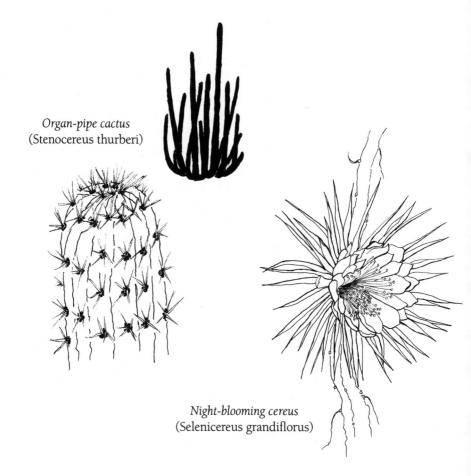

Organ-pipe cactus
(Stenocereus thurberi)

Night-blooming cereus
(Selenicereus grandiflorus)

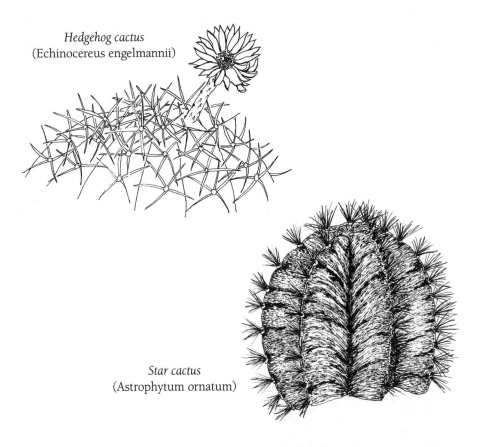

Hedgehog cactus
(Echinocereus engelmannii)

Star cactus
(Astrophytum ornatum)

or cylindrical and have only one joint. It is unusual to find cylinders more than twelve inches long. The color of the spines varies from glassy white to shades of yellow. Although there is a wide variety in the nature of the spines, they are never hooked. Flowers growing on the flat side of the stem give way to spiny fruits. Hedgehog cacti (*Echinocereus engelmannii*) are a popular member of this group. Another genus in this subtribe of interest to the windowsill gardener is *Lobivia*.

Echinocactinae subtribe. The commonly known barrel cacti, in the genera *Echinocactus* and *Ferocactus,* belong to this group. Although some members of this group reach nine to ten feet tall, there are those that make fine houseplants. *Astrophytum* and *Gymnocalycium* don't grow much beyond two feet. Members of this subtribe are covered with hooked spines, are cylindrical with only one joint, and have ribbed stems. Flowers, like cocked hats, grow angled off the stem on areoles. Generally the flowers are small with short tubes. The pronounced ribs and amber spines of the star cactus (*Astrophytum ornatum*) are characteristic of this genus.

Cactaninae subtribe. These are the smallest of the barrel-shaped cacti. Their flowers, which many people say resemble little hats, grow from specialized areoles inside woolly or brushlike projections at the top of the stem. The small melon cactus, or turk's cap *(Melocactus communis),* grows about four to six inches high. Straight, spiny ribs adorn the members of this subtribe. Reddish brown spines and pink flowers are hallmark traits. It takes many years for flowers to develop. Their appearance signals the end of the growth period.

Coryphanthinae subtribe. These cacti have globelike, cylindrical stems covered with bumps or nipples that grow in spirals and take the place of ribs. Spines grow from the top of each nipple. Flowers arise between the bumps or from grooves on them. Some of these cacti belong to the genus *Mammillaria,* frequent members of windowsill gardens. When injured, a watery or milky sap seeps from the wound. The genus *Coryphantha* is another popular member of this subtribe.

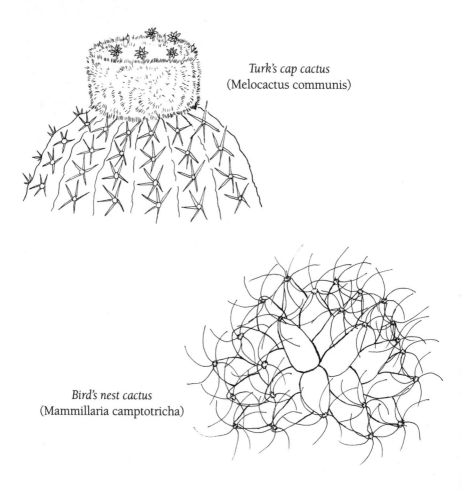

Turk's cap cactus
(Melocactus communis)

Bird's nest cactus
(Mammillaria camptotricha)

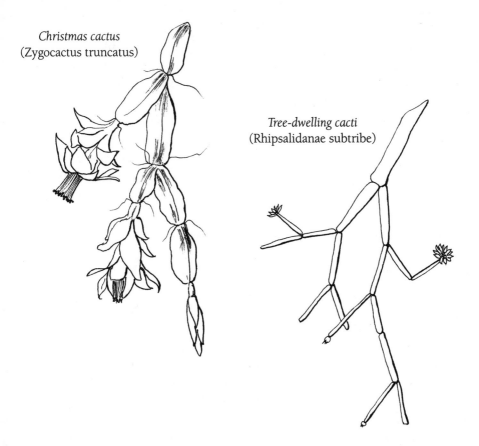

Christmas cactus
(Zygocactus truncatus)

Tree-dwelling cacti
(Rhipsalidanae subtribe)

Epiphyllainae subtribe. These shade-loving plants live on trees in the tropical forests of Central and South America. They have large, colorful, funnel-shaped flowers, many of which are pleasantly scented. The stems are flat but may be angular and have several sides. Even though most lack ribs and spines and some have only bristles and hairs, the presence of areoles in notches along the margins of stems places them in the cactus corner. Hanging baskets suit these plants very well. The Christmas cactus (*Zygocactus truncatus*) is a well-known member of this subtribe. You may know someone who has had good luck with this cactus. They can have stems as long as three feet.

Rhipsalidanae subtribe. Similar to the Epiphyllainae subtribe, members of this group also grow on trees in their native territory. They lack ribs and are spineless, although tufts of hair or bristles come from the areoles on the branches of most species. They are hanging or creeping epiphytes—plants that grow on other plants for support and do not harm the supporting plant. They lack showy flowers, and their fruits are extremely small. Their cascading growth pattern makes them well suited as hanging plants.

EXPLORATIONS

Potting Cacti. With such a wide variety of cacti available, you must get information on potting for each species. Ortho Books, available in the nursery department of home improvement stores, provide helpful information, as does *Landscaping Indoors,* edited by Scott D. Appell and published by the Brooklyn Botanic Garden. What kind of container is best for a particular cactus? Will it grow better in a wide or narrow pot? Rounded cacti, such as the barrel cactus (*Ferocactus acanthodes*) and the old lady cactus (*Mammillaria* sp.), do well in a pot that is only slightly larger than the plant's diameter. Avoid buying tiny cacti sold in tiny pots. There is so little soil in these pots that water drains out quickly, leaving the plant dry shortly after you water it. If possible, visit a nursery that specializes in cacti, and see what criteria the experts use to select an appropriate pot size.

Pots are available in various materials. Clay pots, also known as terra cotta, are pretty and popular, but they are expensive. They come in a variety of sizes, which adds to their versatility. Unless they are glazed, terra cotta pots are porous, so they lose moisture more rapidly than containers of similar size made of a nonporous material. Plastic pots are lightweight, nonporous, relatively inexpensive, and come in a variety of colors. Metal cans from your recycling bin can be had for free and are another practical choice.

Almost any kind of container will work for cacti as long as some basic needs are met. The essential quality is that the container provide adequate drainage so that the soil will remain loosely packed and well aerated. Clay pots generally come with a hole in the bottom for this purpose. Putting a clay shard from a broken pot over the hole prevents the soil from being washed out of the pot but still permits adequate drainage. Small stones or a piece of wire mesh or nylon will also work. When using a container that lacks drainage holes, put a layer of clay shards or small stones in the bottom of the pot.

When you have selected an appropriate container, make sure it is clean. Unless the pots are new, scrub them well, and rinse them in a solution of ten parts water and one part liquid bleach to remove any mold, mildew, pest remains, or other undesirable material left from previous plantings.

To transplant the cactus into your new pot, wear a pair of heavy gloves, preferably leather, to avoid getting stabbed by the spines. *Do not* try to pull the cactus out of the pot with unprotected hands. You can use a pair of kitchen pasta tongs to lift the cactus out of its old pot, or make a strap of folded newspaper long enough to wrap around the body of the cactus, secure the free ends of the strap in one hand, and use the paper sling to lift the cactus from its container. If the soil in the old pot is slightly wet, you should be able to lift the cactus out easily.

Place the cactus in the new pot. Pour soil around the roots, being careful not to damage them. Continue adding soil to the pot, leaving about an inch of space at the top. This will help avoid spillage when watering the plant. Many of the commercially available soil mixes for cacti are very good. Some have a lot of peat moss, which will harden when dry. A recipe for making your own soil mix is simple. It requires one part sand (not from a beach, due to the salt content), one part garden soil, and one part peat moss. This is a time-tested blend that works well.

Some cactus growers suggest covering the top of the soil with a layer of gravel. This prevents the soil from caking up around the plant's roots. They also suggest that you do not water the cactus for a few days after transplanting. Keep it out of direct sun to allow the roots to recover in case they were damaged during the transplanting process.

The Root System. To examine the root system of a cactus, you will have to remove the cactus from its container. Follow the precautions and instructions as outlined above for handling a cactus.

Once you have the cactus out of its pot, gently shake off the soil and examine the roots. How would you describe them? Is there a carrotlike taproot, or is the root system made up of many small roots and rootlets, each with many root hairs? How does this root design benefit the cactus? Draw a picture of the cactus and its roots.

Still wearing heavy gloves, use a sharp knife to carefully cut a slice from the top of the cactus, and lay the piece, cut side down, on a mixture of sand and soil. Check it daily. How long does it take for new roots to grow?

Container Garden. To make a container or dish garden that mimics a desert scene, fill the container about one-third full with gravel to achieve the essential good drainage. A sprinkle of crushed charcoal on top of the gravel helps keep the container fresh and free of mildew. Top this off with a commercial cactus soil, available at some garden centers, filling the container to about one inch from the rim. The different cacti you select to share a container should have similar requirements for water, temperature, and sunlight. To enhance the scene, add a piece of driftwood or some other artifact.

Propagating Cacti

Cuttings. You can add to your cactus collection by taking cuttings. A cutting often produces an improved shape, especially if the growth pattern of the parent plant has become distorted in some way. Be sure to wear heavy gloves and use a sharp knife. Some cutting suggestions are found in the illustrations.

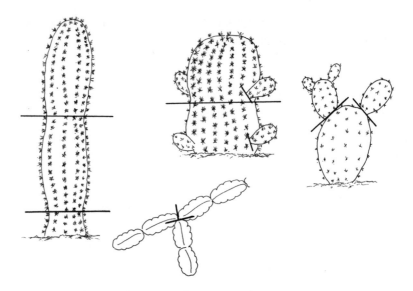

It is best to take cuttings from a natural separation point.

Place the cuttings in a cool, dry area, avoiding direct sunlight, until the wounds have hardened. Depending on the size of the cut, the drying process may take from a few days to several weeks. Next you'll want to plant your cuttings in a commercial cactus soil mixture or sand. Before planting, test the drainage of the soil by running water through the pot; it should drain quickly. If drainage is poor, you can add pebbles to the soil mix. Be sure the cuttings stand upright. To achieve this, you will have to experiment with planting them at different depths in the soil.

Water the cuttings immediately after planting. Too much water is the primary reason for rooting failure, as it causes root rot, so avoid soggy soil. Allow the soil to become totally dry between waterings, but do not let it remain dry for as long as three or four days. For indoor cacti, the drying time may be as short as twenty-four hours.

You will have the best results if you make the cuttings during the natural growing season. In most cases, this is during warm weather.

Grafting. Would you like to have a new cactus that is a product of your imagination? Or perhaps you would simply like to improve a failing cactus in your windowsill garden. Both of these goals are possible through a process called grafting.

When grafting, you attach a stem cut from a plant you want to improve, called the scion, to the root or stem of a vigorous, closely related cactus, called the stock. The best time for this procedure is during the spring or early autumn, when there is sufficient sap flowing. The cactus you select for the stock must have a healthy root system. A good candidate has uniform color and is firm to the touch, not soft or mushy. It's suggested that the stock and the scion be of the same diameter, but a somewhat smaller scion will work as well. The scion will retain its own characteristics but will get its nourishment from the stock's root system.

Using a clean, sharp knife, cut the scion and the stock straight across, on the horizontal, as indicated in the diagram. It's suggested that you bevel the cut edges of the scion and the stock to prevent shrinkage. Press the cut areas of the two pieces together firmly to remove any air that might interfere with the grafting process, and secure them with a rubber band. Keep the grafted cactus out of direct sunlight, and don't water it until you notice the parts beginning to grow together. This may take about four weeks. Cacti that are

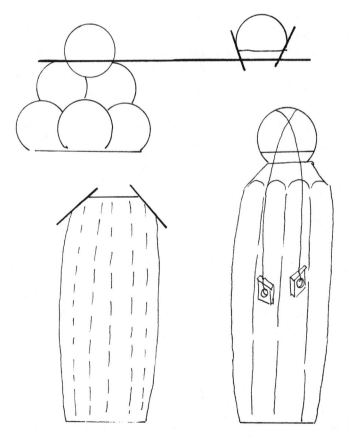

Thick, round scions, commonly astride a column cactus, call for a flat graft, which is the simplest graft.

rounded, such as the members of the *Echinocactus* genus, are best suited for this type of graft. Because of its small size, the hedgehog cactus (*Rebutia* sp.) is another good candidate for the stock, and *Gymnocalycium* sp. makes a good scion.

Keep a record of what you did and how it worked. How does the grafted cactus appear? Does it produce any young sprouts, called offsets? If a cactus produces offsets, detach, plant, and enjoy them.

CHAPTER NOTES

1. There are four distinct desert regions in the western United States. Each has unique features.

a. The Great Basin Desert, at an elevation of four thousand feet, has only scant rainfall that's fairly evenly parceled out during the year. Its cold winters and mild to hot summers support a number of hardy cacti and low shrubs, such as sagebrush and saltbush. It is located within the boundaries of Oregon, Idaho, Nevada, Wyoming, and Utah.

b. The Sonoran Desert is somehat lower in elevation, reaching only about thirty-five hundred feet at its highest point. It boasts a short winter but a hot summer. Rainfall is sparse and comes only during the winter and summer seasons. Saguaro and cholla are the dominant cacti. The Arizona fishhook cactus (*Mammillaria microcarpa*) and the compass cactus (*Ferocactus acanthodes*) are among the many other cacti that find their home in this dry land. Sections of Arizona, Mexico, and southeastern California make up this desert.

c. The Mojave Desert lies between the Great Basin and Sonoran Deserts. Like those deserts, the Mojave experiences cool winters and nearly rainless summers. Shrubs like the creosote bush dominate the landscape, but at higher elevations the Joshua tree flourishes.

d. The Chihuahuan Desert reaches into Arizona, New Mexico, and Texas, but most of its expanse is in Mexico. It is high, with an elevation of greater than thirty-five hundred feet. Known for its broad plateaus, which are refreshed by winter and summer rains, the desert supports grasses, yuccas, agaves, and some small cacti.

2. All succulents have fleshy stems and roots that are capable of storing water. The term *succulent* covers a great variety of plants and does not denote any relationship among them. It merely describes the fleshy nature of some parts of these plants. Succulents of many kinds may have spines, but they do not grow from areoles as do the spines of cacti.

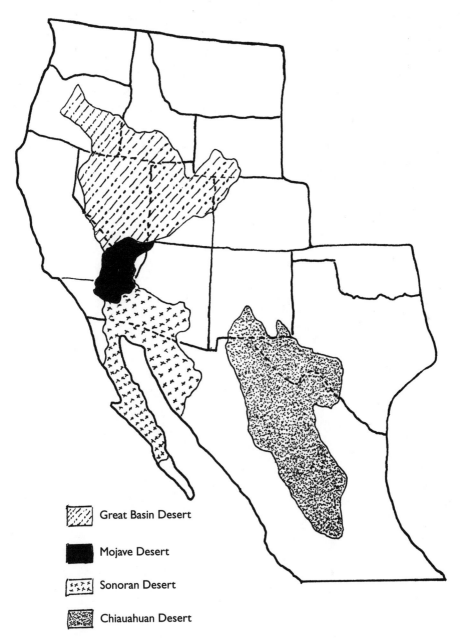

Great Basin Desert

Mojave Desert

Sonoran Desert

Chiauahuan Desert

Map of American deserts

3. If you live near a botanical garden, try to visit it to learn how cacti are grown. To learn the locations of botanical gardens, visit the American Association of Botanical Gardens website, at www.aabga.org, and click on "Member Gardens."

Florists' greenhouses and university or college conservatories that specialize in houseplants are other resources. Additional sources frequently can be found in garden magazines. The Greenlife Gardens, 101 County Line Rd., Griffin, GA 30223, and the Rainbow Gardens, 1444 E. Taylor St., Vista, CA 92084, are two such sources.

4. During the summer months, we wear light-colored clothing to keep us cool by reflecting sunlight—the light-colored spines do the same for cacti.

CHAPTER 3

White Potatoes

WORLD TRAVELERS

In the United States, the potato is ubiquitous. We're tempted by fast-food french fries, we enjoy a bag of potato chips while watching TV, and what would any restaurant be without mashed potatoes on the menu? To the delight of the potato fancier, the potato is cholesterol-free, at least before we load it with toppings like butter or cheese.

Some scientists believe the wild ancestors of today's white potatoes originated along the Chilean coast as many as thirteen thousand years ago, about the time the most recent glacier was receding in North America, and that they were first domesticated some seven thousand years ago on the Andean altiplano. This is remarkable, since life at twelve thousand to fourteen thousand plus feet in elevation would have been rigorous not only for the potatoes, but also for the people who cultivated them. The region's thin atmosphere and summer temperatures that reach into the sixties during the day but hover around the freezing mark at night support very little vegetation. Rainfall in these highlands is minimal and often unpredictable. Crops grown elsewhere as staple foods, such as rice, soybeans, wheat, and corn, could not survive under these conditions.

Nevertheless, different kinds of small, possibly gravel-sized potatoes grew in the varied ecosystems of the jagged, mountainous lands. The exposure to sunlight, rainfall, and wind, as well as soil conditions, differed widely from one location to another. These variables produced potatoes that varied in color, size, and shape. Their colors ranged from white to purple, with many hues in between, such as yellow, blue, black, and even piebald.

Through careful observation, the native people who lived in this rugged environment learned the tricks of successful potato cultivation. They also discovered how to harvest and store the potatoes, which became the staple of their diet. This is not difficult to believe, since scientists have shown that potatoes provide all of the vital nutrients except for calcium and vitamins A and D.

Since its humble beginnings, the potato has had an adventurous life. When the Spanish explorers invaded the land of the Incas, they were looking for gold and silver, which they believed to be there in large quantities. What they did not expect was to discover a food of such nutritional value that it would become a staple in the diets of people around the world. In preparing their ships for the return trips to Spain, the sailors carried potatoes with them. It was a surprise that none of those who ate the vegetable were afflicted with scurvy, a devastating disease brought on by a lack of vitamin C in the diet. In

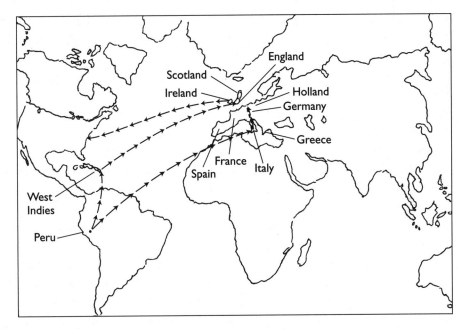

The spread of the humble potato from the altiplano of Peru to Europe and the Americas.

Seville, Spain, the potato found its way into a hospital, where it was used to help treat patients whose illnesses were brought on by dietary deficiencies.

The potato eventually showed up in Italy, France, Greece, Holland, and the rest of Europe, as well as in Russia. It did not quickly become a food for the middle and upper classes, who considered it suitable only as fodder, and certainly not for the elite. However, these attitudes did not stop the march of the potato across the world.

The little spud that grew in the altiplano also landed in the West Indies, and from there it was eventually brought to England, Scotland, and Ireland. Scottish and Irish emigrants who left their homelands and settled in New Hampshire in 1719 became the first potato farmers in North America. In 1845, potatoes in Ireland suffered from a fungal disease brought on by the late blight. This virulent organism ultimately destroyed the crop and caused a famine among the Irish. A million people died from starvation, and many more fled their homeland and immigrated to the United States.

Spores of the late blight fungus attack the leaves of the potato plant, where they produce a network of filmlike filaments called mycelium inside the leaves. Once the fungus has infiltrated the leaves, it is immune to chemical sprays. The only way to stop the destruction is to spray the crop before the spores have germinated. Of course, none of this was known at the time of the infestation of late blight in Ireland.

Once the potato reached North America, it established its reputation as a valued food. Prince Edward Island, Nova Scotia, and other Canadian provinces became major potato producers. The United States, due to the production of potatoes in Maine, Washington, Idaho, and other locations, ultimately became the world's number-one producer of potatoes. In recent times, Russia has moved into the number-one slot, followed by China. The United States is next in line, with India as number four. Potatoes have been doing quite well in backyard gardens across the land. In recent times, they have become a favorite of container gardeners, and it is not unusual to find potato plants growing on urban porches, patios, and even windowsills.

White potatoes belong to the nightshade family (Solanaceae), along with tobacco, tomatoes, eggplant, peppers, jimsonweed, black nightshade, horse nettle, and petunias. The nightshade family has a bad reputation because some of its members, such as jimsonweed, are poisonous to humans. Even the portions of the potato plant that grow above the ground can harm us if eaten, whereas the part that develops below the ground is not only edible, but nutritious. Some nightshade plants are sources of valuable medicines, such as belladonna, digitalis, and atropine. Although many of the nightshade plants differ greatly in their general appearance, these plants have some fascinating similarities.

Consider the petunia. The beauty of its flowers and its relatively easy care make it a favorite patio plant, and many people also have them growing in various other locations around the house. As in all plants in the nightshade group, the petals of the flowers are fused, although the others lack the floppy appearance of the petunia flower. Consistent with other members of the family, the filaments of the stamens, the pollen-producing male organs, are fused to the corolla, the collective term for the flower petals. A close look will reveal these family traits.

Another member of the family, jimsonweed (Datura stramonium), is frequently found growing wild in lots, neglected fields, and even cultivated gardens. It has relatively large, funnel-shaped flowers, but they lack the floppy flare of the petunia. The corolla of the jimsonweed flower is tubelike, wider at the top than at the bottom, and it is unlike the flowers of the tomato and potato.

In similar habitats and in open woods, additional wild members of the family, such as horse nettle (Solanum carolinense) and black nightshade

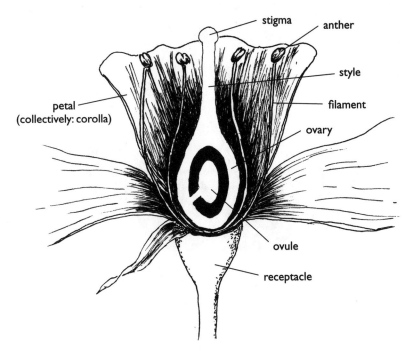

Parts of a typical flower (not the potato flower)
anther + filament = stamen
stigma + style + ovary + ovule = pistil

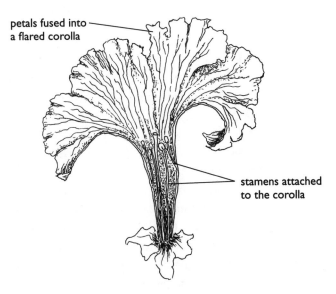

Cross section of a petunia

Potato seeds grow inside the ovary, which changes after the flower dies into a small green fruit that looks like a cherry tomato.

(*Solanum americanum*), might thrive. The flowers of these plants are similar to those of the potato and tomato, with five curved-backward petals exposing the vibrant yellow anthers.

The anthers of potato flowers, along with their filaments, make up the male parts of the flower, or stamens, which are shorter than the pistils, or female parts, which they surround. This design helps prevent the flowers from being fertilized with their own pollen. The yellow pollen on the anthers attracts a variety of insects to feed on the flowers, and in the process, they transport the pollen of one plant to others.

After pollination, a part of the pistil called the ovary swells and ultimately develops into a seed-filled berry that look similar to a small green tomato. When the berries of the potato plant are ripe, they release their seeds, which fall onto the soil. In time, if conditions are right, the seeds will germinate and produce new potato plants.

Potatoes produced by seeds often are very different from either of the parent plants. These new potatoes might have the traits of their "aunts," "uncles," "grandparents," "great-grandparents," or even those of more distant ancestors that grew in the Andean highlands. It is possible for these seed-generated potatoes to come in a variety of colors and shapes. If you were to see corkscrew-shaped, multicolored potatoes at the market, you might wonder if they were to be baked, boiled, or roasted. You might even wonder if they were to be eaten.

Those in the potato industry would wonder how these odd potatoes could be good for chips or fries. Plant scientists have been able to create "improved" potatoes through manipulation of their genetic makeup. Today potatoes can be designed to contain antibiotics and other medicines to treat diseases in underdeveloped countries.

Potatoes can also reproduce through a cloning process called vegetative propagation, a common occurrence in the plant world in which the offspring are genetically identical to each other and to the parent plant. Goldenrod is a familiar plant that reproduces this way. Often you will see various-sized clumps of goldenrod in fields. Each of the plants in the clump is a clone of

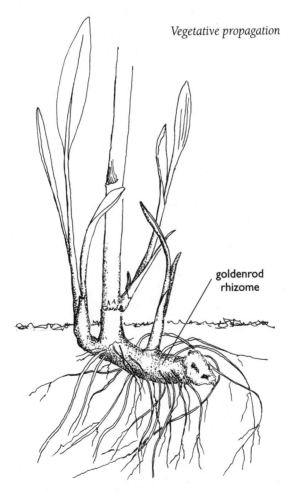

Vegetative propagation

goldenrod
rhizome

Goldenrod reproduces from underground stems or rhizomes sent out by the parent plant.

the parent. Vegetative propagation is a faster and more certain method of reproduction than seed propagation.

Commercial growers use this strategy to their advantage, producing fields of potatoes that are clones of those that have been successful in the marketplace. They can grow these as long as the demand remains. In order to produce these potatoes, the grower uses "seed potatoes," which you will encounter in the activity section of this chapter. The downside of this form of propagation is that if a virus attacks that type of potato, it can become a gigantic disaster for the farmers. Since all of those potatoes have identical disease-fighting strategies, if they are not resistant to that particular virus, the farmer could lose the entire crop.

In addition to viruses and fungi, there are a variety of insect pests that can cause tremendous damage to potato plants. These include aphids and leafhoppers, but the most dreaded of these pests in the United States is the Colorado potato beetle. This is an attractive little scoundrel that used to feed on a plant called sandbur, a relative of the potato that grew in eastern and southern Colorado. With the introduction of the potato, the beetle moved to this more appealing plant and began feeding on its leaves. This activity can quickly reduce a potato field to mere stalks. What makes this pest even more harmful to a potato crop is that it feeds in the larval stage as well as in its adult form.

Today farmers use chemicals to halt the progress of the beetle before it can gain a foothold in their fields. Although chemical warfare may seem like

The Colorado
potato beetle

adult

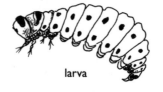

larva

the answer to the problem, insects eventually become immune to chemicals. Fortunately, some beetle watchers have noticed that not only do certain other insects favor the Colorado beetle for a snack, but so do birds such as bob-whites and rose-breasted grosbeaks.

Another vegetable that bears the word *potato* in its name is the sweet potato. Like the white potato, it develops from tuberlike roots, but it belongs to the Convolvulaceae family. This word comes from the Latin *convolvere,* which means "to twine around." If you grow a sweet potato plant, you will see that its vine closely resembles that of the morning glory. You will not see the morning glory–like flowers, however, unless you live in the moist tropics.

Membership in the Convolvulaceae family also is shared by some wild species, such as field bindweed (*Convolvulus arvensis*) and hedge bindweed (*Convolvulus sepium*).

Sweet potatoes originally flourished east of the Andes, but Indian traders took them to Mexico and the Caribbean islands. Columbus is credited with taking the tasty roots to Spain in the late 1400s. In a little more than fifty years, the sweet potato was being grown in the warmer climates of Europe, and before long, people in China, Japan, and the Philippines were enjoying these moist, sweet vegetables.

THE WORLD OF WHITE POTATOES

What you will need	Science skills
a variety of potatoes	observing
plant container	classifying
potting soil	inferring
flowerpots	
iodine	
scale in ounces	

OBSERVATIONS

Potato Flowers. Flowers with five backward-arching petals appear on potato plants when the tuber below the ground is developing. Another notable feature of potato flowers is the yellow beak formed by the fusion of the flower's pistil with the stamens surrounding it. Potatoes that you grow in containers may not produce flowers, but you may see flowers on plants in a commercial

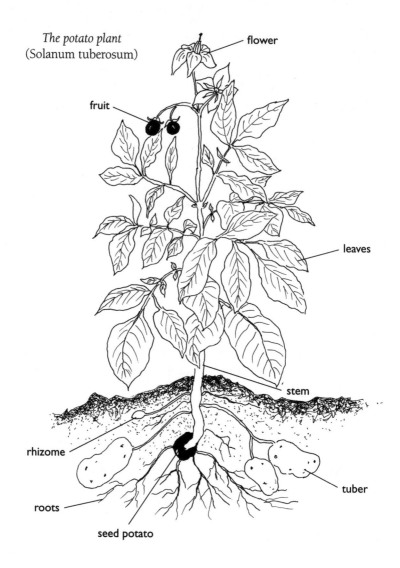

The potato plant
(Solanum tuberosum)

flower

fruit

leaves

stem

rhizome

tuber

roots

seed potato

potato field. However, there are thousands of plants in that field, and relatively few of them will have flowers.

The blossoms are often white, but they also may be shades of blue and purple. By harvest time, the flowers have withered, and the leaves and stems have lost much of their green color. If you are unable to find a potato flower to examine, a flower from a tomato plant will provide similar information about the flower's structure.

An interesting feature that botanists use to classify plants is the position of the flower's ovary in relation to the flower's sepals (known collectively as the calyx). The ovaries of flowers in the nightshade family are positioned

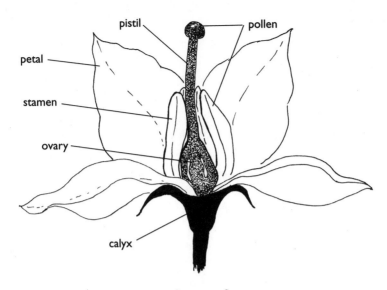

Parts of a potato flower

above the calyx and are referred to as superior ovaries. Plants belonging to other families have different arrangements. For example, the position of the ovaries in apples is considered inferior, while that of cherries is half-inferior. Look for the ovary on the potato or tomato flower. What is its position relative to the calyx? Examine flowers on other plants and see if you can determine the type of ovary each of them has: superior, inferior, or half-inferior. Which do you most often find?

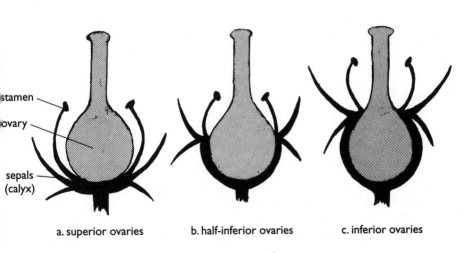

a. superior ovaries   b. half-inferior ovaries   c. inferior ovaries

Ovary positions in flowers

Family Tree. Botanists organize potatoes and other plants according to family, genus, and species. A family of plants includes those that have similar genetic traits but cannot interbreed. Although petunias, potatoes, jimsonweed, horse nettle, black nightshade, and eggplant are members of the Solanaceae (nightshade) family, they cannot share their genes with each other. The next subdivision in the classification system is the genus (plural: genera), a taxonomic group of very similar plants considered to be more closely related than those that make up a family. The next classification is species. The white potato's genus and species are *Solanum tuberosum*. Within the species there are several varieties, such as russet Burbanks, Norgold russets, and reds.

Characteristics of White Potatoes. The most common potatoes are white, red, and russet. These are collectively called white or Irish white potatoes. These are the potatoes commonly eaten baked, boiled, mashed, and as french fries and chips.

Make a trip to the produce section of a market and buy a few each of white, red, and russet potatoes. Which of these potatoes is most common in your market? Visit other markets to see if there is a different pattern to the kind of potatoes you find. Keep an eye on the potato section as you visit the market over the course of a year. Is the frequency of one type of potato a seasonal event, or do different types of white potatoes appear randomly?

At home, examine the characteristics that identify each of these types of potatoes. What is the color of the skin? How would you describe its texture—is it smooth or rough? Does it have a pattern on it? Describe the shapes of the potatoes. Are they round, oval, or oblong? Record your information on a chart similar to this one:

Variety	Skin Color	Skin Texture	Shape	Frequency Found
white				
red				
russet				

Cut the potatoes in half. Examine the flesh of each kind of potato. Describe it. What similarities do you notice? Differences?

Potato Size. When you buy a sack of potatoes at the supermarket, you may notice that they are all about the same size. How does this happen?

Commercial growers grade potatoes by a variety of techniques. One is to group potatoes according to their weight. According to this test, large potatoes weigh between ten and sixteen ounces, medium potatoes are more than five ounces but less than ten ounces, and small potatoes are those less than five ounces. Examine the contents of a five-pound bag of potatoes. Weigh each potato. What did you find out? How many small, medium, and large potatoes were in the bag?

Potato Eyes. Each potato eye is a node that forms around a modified stem. A node is a region of a stem where one or more leaves are attached. Select a potato. How many eyes does it have? Examine all the eyes of the potato. Do you see any sign of a sprout? Immature leaves? Do your other potatoes have the same number of eyes? More? Less? How many buds can you see in each eye? A seed potato can have just one eye, but two to four eyes are preferred.

You will see that there is a cluster of eyes at one end of the potato. This is referred to as the eye end of the potato. The other end of the potato is the stem end. Look on this end for the attachment scar where the potato was attached to the stem.

Some potatoes have shallow eyes, and others have deep eyes. The potato chip industries prefer potatoes with very shallow eyes. Are the eyes of your potatoes deep or shallow?

Above the eyes, potatoes have eyebrows. Look carefully; you may never have noticed the eyebrows before. How are they oriented on the potato? Are they all positioned in the same direction?

Potato Sprouts. Examine your potatoes for sprouts, thick, yellow-white objects protruding from the eyes. Look closely and you may see young, folded leaves. Sometimes the sprout is not very long and simply resembles a small bump in the skin. Look at the base of the sprout for rhizomes (underground stems) and small roots. With the help of a hand lens, you may be able to see delicate root hairs growing off the roots. In time, the tips of the rhizomes will swell and become a tuber—a new potato. Do all the eyes have sprouts?

Potato Pests. The Colorado potato beetle is the most feared potato pest in North America, but if you are growing your potatoes in a container indoors, you probably will not have to worry about it. However, some Homoptera, such as aphids, leafhoppers, psyllids, and other sucking insects, can become a problem even indoors. These insects use their sharp mouthparts to pierce and suck fluids from the leaves and stems. Another potato pest is the potato psyllid (*Paratrioza cockerelli*).

EXPLORATIONS

Growing Potatoes from Seed Potatoes. If you want to grow a potato the way commercial growers cultivate them, you will need to have a seed potato. Finding one is not difficult. Sometimes all you need to do is look in a recently

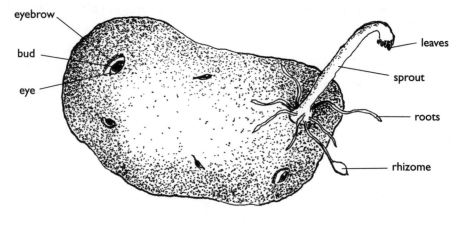

eyebrow

bud

eye

leaves

sprout

roots

rhizome

A sprouting potato

bought bag of potatoes, and you will see a few potatoes that are beginning to sprout. Failing to find a seed potato in the bag, there is another surefire technique. Sometimes one or more of the bagged potatoes escapes from the bag and gets pushed to the back of the storage cabinet. One day you reach into that cabinet and find the lost spud only to discover some strange yellowish shoots and some long, threadlike strands (the rhizomes) growing from it. Usually there is more than one of these sprouts on the potato. This is what is known as a "seed potato," although it really doesn't have any seeds. It is so called because it contains all the necessary ingredients to produce potatoes identical to itself.

Once you have obtained such a potato, cut off several pieces with two or three eyes on each. Cut two or three more pieces that have no eyes. Using a large flowerpot for each piece, plant them in soil to a depth of about three inches. Use sterile potting soil, which can be bought in a nursery or supermarket. How long does it take the sprouts, now the stem, of the new plants, to poke through the soil? Did all your potato pieces grow stems?

When a plant has become tall and leaves are present, remove it from the pot, along with the ball of soil. You will see underground rhizomes, and maybe even a tiny potato or two. Look for the original piece of seed potato. How has it changed since you planted it?

If you want the plant to continue to grow, replant it in a larger pot or outdoors to allow room for more growth. You might eventually be able to eat the potatoes you grow.

Cooking White Potatoes. In general, the three types of white potatoes are cooked by different methods: Russets are baked, reds are boiled, and whites are mashed. Prepare each type of potato according to its preferred use, but do not add anything to them, such as butter or milk. Compare the flesh of each before and after cooking. How do they differ? Are there any similarities? Eat some of each cooked potato. How would you describe the taste and texture of each different potato? Is it slightly sweet or bland? Is it smooth, dry, soft? Invite some friends to try the taste test with you.

Boiled red potatoes have been described as slightly sweet, russets bland and soft, and whites bland and dry. How do your findings stand against these evaluations?

How each kind of potato is used is also dictated by the amount of glucose and dry matter it contains. Red potatoes have a high concentration of glucose and are preferred for boiling and use in potato salads. But red potatoes are not firm enough for french fries or potato chips. Russets have an intermediate glucose content, and such potatoes make the best french fries. Whites are low in glucose and high in dry matter, and as such, they are good for making potato chips.

Have you ever tried using russet potatoes for salad or baking a red potato? How did you like the results? How do cookbooks make use of this information?

Glucose Content. At a pharmacy, buy a container of Chem-Strip, used to test the urine of diabetics, or TesTape, which is used to test for the glucose content in blood. You will also need a selection of red, white, and russet potatoes.

Cut each potato to be tested lengthwise, and place a length of a glucose test strip on one half of the potato. Do not touch the strip except at each end. Put the other potato half on top, and press the two halves together briefly. Remove the strip immediately, and wait one minute.

If the potato is low in glucose, the strip will remain yellow. For the commercial world, this means the potato will "fry light." If the strip is green, find out how much glucose there is in the potato by comparing the color of the strip with the chart that came with the package. If the strip indicates 0.2 percent glucose or greater, the potatoes will "fry dark." What did you find out about the three different kinds of potatoes? This information is important for people in the potato chip industry. How do you like your chips?

Greening of a Potato. Select about eight potatoes of the same type and size. Put four of them in direct sunlight and the other four in a dark place for several weeks. Check on them periodically. When you notice a greenish color on one of the potatoes left in the sunlight, cut off a slice and measure the amount of green. How long did it take for the potato to start greening?

Examine those left in the dark. Is there any evidence of green on those potatoes? Slice all of the potatoes, and determine the amount of green, or lack of it, in each.

The green color is caused by chlorophyll manufactured by the potato. The potatoes that are still alive respond to their exposure to sunlight by photosynthesizing. The parenchyma cells that once held food and water have begun storing chlorophyll.

Growing Sweet Potatoes. To grow a sweet potato plant, you need a sweet potato that is producing buds. In the market, look for sweet potatoes that show some signs of life, such as buds in the eyes. They may or may not have some roots emerging from them. It is often difficult to find such a sweet potato, because many of those you find in markets have been heat-dried in order to protect them from spoilage. If you persist in your search, however, you will eventually find a good subject. There are two main planting methods:

1. In a large flowerpot, place the whole sweet potato horizontally on top of moist sand, and cover with sand to a depth of about one inch. Give it lots of water, but not so much that you create puddles in the sand. After a few weeks, sprouts will appear. When they are about six inches tall, remove the sweet potato from the sand. Pull off each sprout, and plant them separately in potting soil in individual flowerpots.

2. An alternate method requires a glass of water, three toothpicks, and a sweet potato. Insert the toothpicks into the potato about one-third of the way from the rounded end. Fill the glass almost to the top with water, and put the narrow end of the sweet potato into the water so that the toothpicks support it on the rim of the glass.

How long does it take the sweet potato to sprout? How quickly does the vine grow? Measure the length every other day, and keep a record of the growth in your journal. On average, how much does it grow each day?

CHAPTER NOTE

Many of these activities have been drawn from two articles by Dr. Alexander D. Pavlista in *The American Biology Teacher* 59, no. 1 (January 1997): 30–34.

PART II
THE ANIMALS

CHAPTER 4

Daddy Longlegs

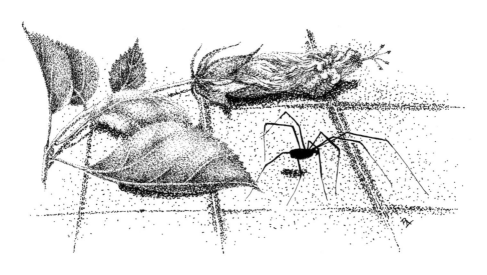

DELICATE DANCERS

One evening late in the summer, I heard the excited voice of a six-year-old visitor at my home declare that she had found a "long daddy legs" speeding across the patio bricks. Not only had she found the spindly creature, but soon it was walking across her outstretched hands, causing even more excitement. It was time to find a suitable jar and a hand lens. Once this strange-looking "spider" was safely secured in the jar and ventilation holes were made in the lid, a litany of questions flowed from my curious visitor.

Due to their spiderlike appearance, daddy longlegs are often confused with spiders. Some people have handled this puzzle by simply calling the long-legged creatures "pseudo spiders." It's easy to see how this confusion developed. Let's take a closer look at these two similar-looking creatures.

Spiders and daddy longlegs both belong to a very large group, the phylum Arthropoda. Arthropods are animals that have a hard external covering or skeleton that protects their soft internal body parts. Another characteristic required for membership in this fraternity is repeating pairs of jointed legs. It is this quality, so obvious in spiders and daddy longlegs, that has caused people to erroneously assume a very close kinship. The large phylum Arthropoda contains about 80 percent of all living creatures. The animals in it belong to one of three classes: crustaceans, insects, and arachnids. Lobsters and crabs are crustaceans; flies, mosquitoes, grasshoppers, and butterflies are a few of the insects; and arachnids include spiders, daddy longlegs, mites, and ticks.

Traits easily seen in the arachnids are the absence of antennae and a body with two divisions: the abdomen and the cephalothorax, a fused head and chest. Scientists who study the arachnids divide them into two subgroups: the Araneae, which contains the spiders, and the Opiliones, or Phalangida, which includes daddy longlegs (see Chapter Note 1).

Spiders have a pedicel, or "waist," that separates the cephalothorax from the abdomen. In the daddy longlegs, these parts are broadly joined, an arrangement that makes the body resemble a Rice Krispies kernel bouncing along on wiry legs. Daddy longlegs have two small mouthparts, called pedipalps, without fangs in front of the mouth, whereas the pedipalps of spiders are each equipped with a pair of double-jointed mouthparts, of which the second segments form hollow fangs. Through these fangs, the spider injects venom into its prey. Once the prey is immobilized, the spider injects an enzyme that converts the interior of the hard-bodied prey into a nutritious soup, which the spider then sucks up. Lacking these special tools, a daddy longlegs must find reasonably soft prey that it can crush with a pair of delicate pincers and then push into its mouth, a small slit at the front end.

A spider (left) has a waist, or pedicel, that separates the cephalothorax from the abdomen. Daddy longlegs (right) have no constriction or waist between thorax and abdomen. Drawing not to scale.

Now you know how spiders and daddy longlegs differ, and why you won't be bitten by a daddy longlegs. Few people ever see a daddy longlegs attack an insect, so they don't have the fearful reputation of spiders. But even though they don't have fanged mouthparts, which might make them a danger to people, they are predators. Daddy longlegs prefer a meal of wingless springtails (see Chapter Note 2). When springtails are not available, they will eat other soft-bodied insects and their larvae. Daddy longlegs are also predators of snails, flies, and aphids, those plant pests that plague indoor and outdoor gardeners. If necessary, daddy longlegs will dine on their own kind, but only occasionally will they attack spiders. Researchers have discovered that daddy longlegs are predatory in soybean and potato fields, finding prey such as small earthworms and a variety of insect eggs to their liking. Soil litter offers additional nutrient value for the hungry daddy longlegs that scavenge for food.

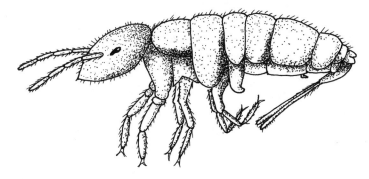

Springtails, minute wingless insects, occur in soil, in leaf litter, under bark, and in similar situations. Most are smaller than 6 mm.

As long as the food is soft, it doesn't matter to the daddy longlegs if it is dead or alive. After all, protein is protein.

Perhaps the most characteristic feature of spiders is their webs and the silk they produce to spin them. In this respect, daddy longlegs are very different, lacking the silk glands required to produce the silk for webs.

Most spiders have four to eight simple eyes, although some have only two, and there are also spiders without any eyes that live in dark caves. Many spiders don't need good eyesight, because they work at night. Those that are active during the day have better vision.

Daddy longlegs have only one pair of eyes, each mounted on a stalklike structure on the top of the cephalothorax. They do not see well. Shadows and movement are the most they can detect with their eyes, but they have an interesting strategy that takes the place of acute vision. They use two of their eight legs as feelers that incorporate three senses: touch, taste, and smell. They probably "hear" by feeling substrate vibrations.

The most obvious characteristic that daddy longlegs share with spiders is their four pairs of jointed legs. These legs give members of both groups dexterity and agility, but those of the daddy longlegs have some additional qualities. If you look closely at one of these delicate dancers, you will notice that the second pair of legs is significantly longer than the others. This pair of legs is extremely important. These are the legs used as feelers for touching, smelling, and tasting. Except when running, a daddy longlegs waves them almost constantly, because they provide the creature with sensory information about the environment.

This pair of legs is so important that the daddy longlegs will clean them several times a day. If you spend some time watching a daddy longlegs, you might be lucky enough to witness the procedure.

If a predator should grab onto a leg, the daddy longlegs will release it. The leg remains with the predator and continues to wiggle, serving as a distraction that allows the daddy longlegs time to escape. Children playing with this harmless creature soon discover this leg-shedding behavior.

Daddy longlegs cannot grow new legs to replace these lost ones, as can some spiders, such as tarantulas or brown recluses. What chemicals the daddy longlegs lacks to make a new leg remain unknown. This is of little consequence, as long as one of the second pair remains intact. The loss of both legs of this pair signals doom. No longer able to detect an approaching predator, the daddy longlegs soon will become a meal. Large insects, birds, and toads head the list of those that find daddy longlegs particularly tasty, although the creature's speed and protective coloration combine to save it from many hunters.

In addition, an unpleasant secretion from specialized scent glands behind the front legs effectively repels some unwelcome advances. Generally, humans are unable to detect this odor, but scientists who have worked closely with daddy longlegs say they can easily identify various species by their distinctive odors.

Although daddy longlegs require some water, they need very little, so it is not surprising to find them in dry areas in and around your house. What little water they need is usually absorbed from the food they eat and from morning dew, although you may see daddy longlegs drinking from puddles. If you look closely, you will see that they actually walk on the water's surface while taking a drink.

Daddy longlegs mate in the fall. The male and female begin touching each other with their second pair of legs before actually mating. Before winter arrives, adult females lay as many as forty tiny, pale green eggs. It is important that she deposit her eggs where they can be protected from the cold. Wood-piles, leaf litter, even a mound of rags in your garage are suitable places for the eggs to overwinter. From these, hatchlings about the size of the head of a pin emerge, but they will not mature until the following spring. Perhaps you will find their haven beneath a woodpile on a porch or in the leaf litter that accumulates in a window well, where they will keep warm throughout the cold season. As the weather warms, you may see them running along the ground near a downspout, by a cellar window, or even inside your house.

These tiny creatures have a lot to do in a very short time to keep their species going, so they grow quickly. About an hour after they are born, they shed their first skin. These molts continue until they reach adult size. The actual number of molts depends on the species, but it's in the neighborhood of seven. Although the skin that is shed is difficult to find, you might come across one and think it's a tiny dead daddy longlegs. Take a close look. You might be surprised.

Not all daddy longlegs die in the fall following their birth. One species in the South lives through the winter as an adult and keeps warm buried beneath leaf litter. This group lays its eggs in the spring. In the warmer parts of the United States and in the tropics, the long-legged variety is replaced by a short-legged group. Those living in the warmer climates do not move as rapidly as their northern cousins.

Daddy longlegs are also known in the United States as harvestmen. The French call them harvest makers, and the English refer to them as harvest spiders. These names apparently come from their habit of gathering in large numbers during harvest time in late summer and early autumn. At this time, you can find very large groups of them amassing on plant material and tree trunks. Sometimes they are seen in large aggregations with their legs entangled. This behavior is thought to be a strategy for keeping warm.

Daddy longlegs are common, with about two hundred species thriving throughout the United States and in parts of Canada, but their abundance has not led to a deep understanding of them. We know relatively little about daddy longlegs. The scientists who have dedicated their time and energy to learning more about them receive little funding to support their efforts, which may be because daddy longlegs don't cause us or our pets or our edible crops any diseases, nor do they offer cures for any of the diseases that plague us.

When you find these rapid runners scurrying over blades of grass and along the screens of your porch or in the garage, you may wonder about the secrets they hold. Certainly you can enjoy watching these agile creatures in their determination to get where they are going, and only they know where that may be.

THE WORLD OF DADDY LONGLEGS

What you will need	Science skills
basic kit	observing
patience	comparing
	inferring

OBSERVATIONS

The cool nights and warm days of autumn bring daddy longlegs out of hiding, and this is the best time for a productive arachnid hunting season. Daddy longlegs are not as easy to track down as spiders (see Chapter Note 3). Most of the time they just appear. If you are working in the garden or at your desk, you may suddenly find a daddy longlegs close by. They are silent and may startle you. To find a daddy longlegs, look in a garage or barn, on the porch or patio, or even in your house. You might find them running along the tops of shrubs and other plantings around your house, or among the cobwebs that tend to accumulate in basements and garages. When trapping a daddy longlegs, be sure your container is large enough to accommodate its long, wispy limbs.

Kinds of Daddy Longlegs. There are several kinds of daddy longlegs. The one you are most likely to find around the house is the brown daddy longlegs (*Phalangium opilio*). It is small, with a reddish brown body that may reach a

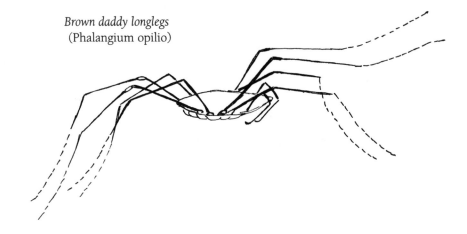

Brown daddy longlegs
(Phalangium opilio)

quarter inch. It has two eyes on black turrets. Although its eyes see only shadows, one eye scans to the right while the other eye looks left. It is not very fussy about living in places that we have disturbed. It is even comfortable in places we have made quite messy.

The eastern daddy longlegs (*Leiobunum* sp.) is very common. You can expect to find them on shady outside walls of buildings. Their second pair of legs has been recorded as sometimes being up to fifteen times the length of the body. Look for a brown body with a yellow-green hue.

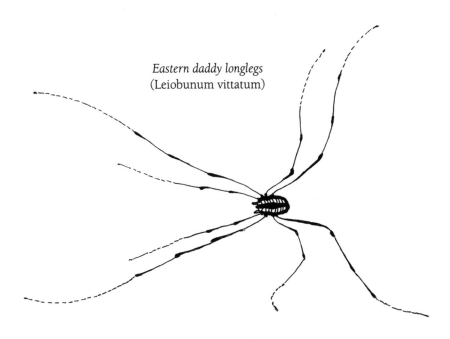

Eastern daddy longlegs
(Leiobunum vittatum)

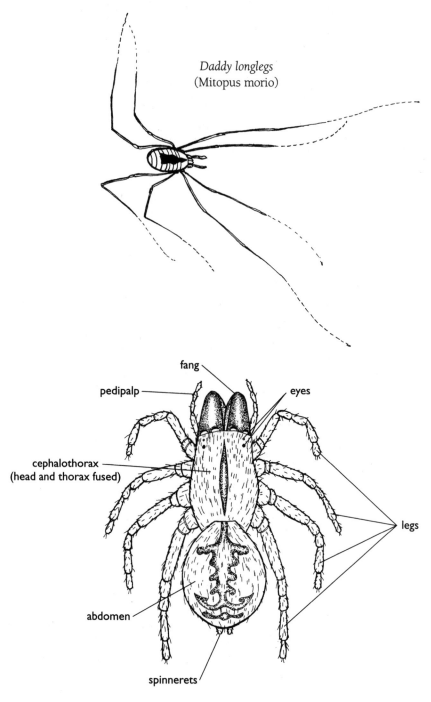

Daddy longlegs
(Mitopus morio)

fang

pedipalp

eyes

cephalothorax
(head and thorax fused)

legs

abdomen

spinnerets

Anatomy of a spider

Another common and widespread daddy longlegs is *Mitopus morio,* identified by the black stripe on top of the cephalothorax. Other species include *Leiobunum vittatum,* which appears all across the country, and the dark brown *Hadrobunus maculosus,* which lives mostly in the Northeast.

Find several daddy longlegs and compare them with each other. Look for similarities and differences. Do you have different species?

Daddy Longlegs Hideouts. Describe the places where you found the daddy longlegs. Were they dry, damp, or wet? Did you find them hiding in direct sunlight, or were the places shaded or dark? What was the temperature in the hideouts? Were the conditions similar in the hideouts of the different daddy longlegs you found?

Daddy Longlegs versus Spiders. With the help of the diagrams in this chapter, compare a daddy longlegs with a captured spider (keep them in different containers). Look for similarities and differences between these two arachnids. Record your observations in your notebook. A chart similar to the one below may be helpful. Add any other comparisons that you observe.

	Daddy Longlegs	Spider
Legs		
segments		
joints		
hairs		
points of attachment		
Body		
color, top and underside		
segments		
pedicel ("waist")		
hairs		
Head		
eyes		
hairs		
mouthparts		

Legs. As you examine the daddy longlegs, keep in mind that a detached leg is a leg lost forever, so handle it carefully. Where the legs are attached to the body of the daddy longlegs and the spider, do the points of attachment appear the same? How many joints are there in each leg? How many segments? Are all the segments of equal length? How are the legs of the spider similar to or different from the legs of the daddy longlegs?

How would you describe the daddy longlegs' second pair of legs? How much longer are they than the other legs? When the daddy longlegs is at rest, what does it do with the second pair of legs?

You may find a daddy longlegs that is missing one or more of its legs. Can you see where the leg broke off? Was it at the joint nearest the body, the joint farthest from the body, or somewhere in between?

Body. How would you describe the shape of the daddy longlegs' body? What is the color? How does this offer protection to the daddy longlegs? Is the color the same on the top and the underside? Are there any markings on the body? If so, describe them. Make similar observations about the spider.

Look for four tiny bumps on the underside of the body of the daddy longlegs. Each leg is attached to one of these bumps. Sensory organs are in this area as well.

Daddy Longlegs Behavior. When at rest, how does the daddy longlegs stand? The spider? Draw a picture of each at rest. Describe the movement of their bodies when they walk or run. Describe the position of the body relative to the legs. Is the body always level with the knees?

As you spend time observing a daddy longlegs, you will see it position its body below its "knees." When in this position, it can be seen pumping its body up and down. Some arachnologists, those who study spiders and their relatives, think this happens when the daddy longlegs is frightened or when it is in a mating mood.

Daddy longlegs are extremely clean. They must keep their legs free of dust, pollen, and other debris that might interfere with their daily activity. They do this by grooming, or preening. To accomplish the job, a daddy longlegs threads a leg through its mouth, holding it in place until the tip is reached. Then the leg springs back into place. The process cleans important sensory receptors on the legs and may also prevent the legs from drying out. This is a behavior you can observe, although it will take patience, persistence, and some luck. Record the process and make a drawing of it.

Molt. A daddy longlegs sheds its first skin within the first hour after hatching. In response to chemical signals, it finds something suitable to hang onto with its fourth pair of legs. On schedule, its skin slits down the back, and each leg in turn is slowly drawn out of the old skin. When empty, the old skin is left dangling. Daddy longlegs shed every ten days, a total of five to nine times, before fully grown. Because these molted skins are so small and fragile, they are extremely difficult to find. If you do find one, describe the skin and where you found it in your notebook.

EXPLORATIONS

Group Behavior. Put two or three daddy longlegs in a small, eight-ounce jar. Observe them for a period of time. What do they do? Now put them in a large jar with enough room for each to move freely. How do they behave under these conditions? Do the daddy longlegs stay close to each other, or do they seem to spend most of the time separated? How long did it take for them to settle down? How long do they stay in this settled position?

When the daddy longlegs were put in the smaller jar, you probably noticed that they "played dead" after they ran around the jar for a short time. This is called the "narcotic effect." When you move them to a larger jar, they revive almost immediately and become quite active. There have been several tentative explanations for this, but no definitive explanation for the effect they have on each other.

Terrarium. In order to observe daddy longlegs more closely, you can keep one on a temporary basis in a five- or ten-gallon terrarium. Add a few inches of soil and some decaying leaves. If you collect these materials from a woodland or garden, it will contain enough tiny soil organisms to feed the daddy longlegs for a period of time. They require little water. Most of what they need they will take from the soil. Keep it moist by using a spray bottle. Cover the terrarium with plastic wrap or a piece of cardboard. Puncture ventilation holes in this covering.

Do not put the terrarium with its captive in direct sunlight. Heat will build up to dangerous levels, putting the daddy longlegs in serious danger of drying out and dying.

Daddy longlegs often prey on each other, so it is not advisable to keep more than one in a container for an extended period. You can introduce another and leave it for a short time while you make some observations. How does the original tenant behave in the presence of the newcomer?

As you observe the daddy longlegs in captivity, record in your journal what it does. What does it spend most of its time doing: eating, drinking, or preening?

Activities and Responses. If you touch a daddy longlegs, does it scurry away, play dead, or not change its activity at all? How does the daddy longlegs respond to a loud noise? A bright light in a dark room?

Daddy longlegs are equipped with a pair of jaws that can tear food. In front of the first pair of legs is a pair of pedipalps, jointed appendages that hold the soft food while a pair of jawlike structures pulls the food into the mouth. Put a daddy longlegs on your hand along with a drop of water or some food. You might see its mouthparts groping as it searches for the food or water. This will not harm you. Record your observations in your journal.

Touch the daddy longlegs' second pair of legs with a soft object, such as a piece of cotton, as they wave about. Let the legs touch a small piece of cooked, chopped meat. How does the daddy longlegs respond to these objects?

How Fast Can They Go? Anyone who has seen a daddy longlegs in motion will agree that they are fast runners, but just how fast they travel is not generally known.

On a patio or wide driveway, release the daddy longlegs near the center of the pavement. When it starts to run, begin timing. A stopwatch is good for this, although a wristwatch with a second hand can do the job. Use a tape measure to determine how far it traveled in fifteen seconds and thirty seconds. Repeat this several times. What is its average speed per minute? Does it travel in a straight line?

You may have to try this several times to become accustomed to the daddy longlegs' behavior and speed.

CHAPTER NOTES

I. Mites, ticks, and scorpions have a close kinship with daddy longlegs, although they are more closely related to spiders. They all lack antennae, have eight legs, and two body parts.

2. During the warming days of February, snow around tree trunks seems to come alive. Pepperlike specks on the snow appear and then disappear. The movement occurs so swiftly that you might say that the surface of the snow seems fluid, but you are witnessing the surface activity of springtails.

Wingless springtails (*Achorutes nivicola*) belong to a very old and established line of insects called Collembola, which originated before wings had evolved. From an evolutionary point of view, Collembola have been highly successful. The measure of success for any living species is simple: Each generation needs to survive long enough to reproduce. If this short-term success is maintained over a long duration, such as 100 million years, we can say that the species is highly successful.

3. Although spiders are found almost anywhere, the easiest way to locate one is to find its web. Spiders frequently stay close to their webs, and with patience, a lidded jar, and a hand lens, you can usually get a good look at them.

Spider webs vary in design, depending on the spiders that built them:

a. Small grass spiders build funnel webs. The top of the web is a flat sheet and the bottom is shaped like a funnel: wide at one end and narrow at the other. Look for them in grass and low bushes in the early morning.

b. Orb webs are the webs most people associate with spiders; they appear inside barns, inside and outside houses, and on shrubs. Several hundred types of spiders create orb webs, the most common of which is the black and yellow *Argiope*.

c. A prey-catching tangle of threads is produced by the American house spider. Look for these in your basement.

Praying Mantises

AMBUSH PREDATORS

On a tranquil day in late summer, it was resting on the windowsill in your bedroom. Or perhaps you first saw it perched on your sleeve as you sat quietly on the porch reading a magazine. Wherever you had your first encounter with the creature that silently entered your world, it looked like an alien beamed down from a distant starship. While poised with its front legs clasped in a reverent posture, it stared at you with large eyes set in its triangular face, giving the impression it knew all about you. The experience was unsettling. What was it? Where did it come from? Where had it been? And why was it in your living space?

Many people assume these creatures are part of a migratory flock of some foreign creatures on their way from somewhere going to somewhere else. In truth, they are praying mantises, and they have been with us since June, when they hatched from eggs that wintered firmly attached to assorted twigs in fields and gardens. We are rarely aware of mantises until late summer or early autumn. Even then, they go unnoticed much of the time because of their protective coloration—greens, tans, and browns that allow them to blend in with plant foliage. In addition to camouflage, praying mantises use a behavioral strategy called cryptic posturing as a way to remain inconspicuous. To achieve this, the mantis extends its forelegs vertically and grabs onto a stick or blade of grass, which it resembles, making it less visible. In the natural world, this protective mechanism is unusual, and few creatures demonstrate it.

The mantis is a slow-moving insect whose legs are not built for jumping or high-speed running in search of a meal. However, it has evolved into a stellar predator due to some very effective adaptations.

As an insect, a praying mantis has three pairs of legs. Its front legs are larger than the other two pairs and are made of five segments. Two of these segments are armed with spines designed to interlock with each other when the legs come together. The spines do a superb job for the mantis when it is grasping prey. Once caught and held by the interlocking spines, no matter how hard the captive struggles, it cannot free itself from the hold the mantis has on it. These front legs are further distinguished by greatly elongated coxae, the segments that attach to the body. This permits the mantis to move its legs freely and have an extended reach. Although the coxae are present in other insects, they are generally much shorter and stubbier.

Another feature unique to the mantis is its long, necklike structure, in reality an elongated first segment of the thorax. This also aids in catching prey by allowing the mantis to extend its reach. Armed with anatomical advan-

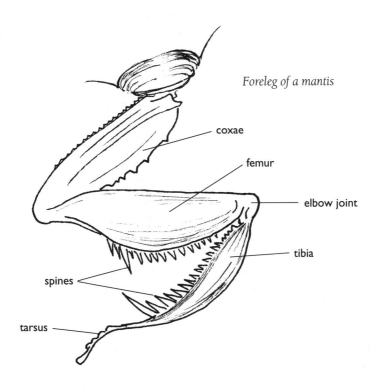

Foreleg of a mantis

coxae

femur

elbow joint

tibia

spines

tarsus

tages such as these, a mantis need only wait for an insect to fly within the scope of its reach and pluck it out of the air.

Large eyes are another hallmark of these fascinating insects. Because of the position of the eyes on the head, mantises have binocular vision, which makes judging distance possible—a distinct advantage for a predator.

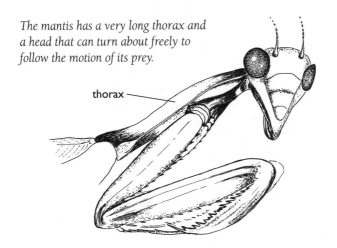

The mantis has a very long thorax and a head that can turn about freely to follow the motion of its prey.

thorax

Another feature that distinguishes the praying mantis from other insects is a movable head that can rotate approximately 180 degrees—another advantage when looking for prey. This capability ranks them as the only insects that can move their heads the way we do.

There are moments when insects or spiders are not so cooperative and come to rest beyond the reach of those fabulous forearms. To capture such prey, the mantis begins a "dance" that is worth watching. The mantis stares at the insect with its commanding heart-shaped eyes and begins a slow, swaying motion. As it continues this motion, the mantis moves very slowly toward the unsuspecting prey. When close enough, its forearms grab the insect and clamp it between the unforgiving spines, and the mantis has its meal.

Mantises are classified as ambush predators. The ambush is one of three techniques predatory insects use to capture prey. The ambush bug behaves similarly to the mantis in securing its meals, lying in wait for its prey. It too has spines on its large forelegs. Another food-getting strategy is referred to as searching. Dragonflies use this method, cruising the air in their hunt for mosquitoes and other flying insects. The third method used to capture food is called trapping. It is illustrated by ant lions, which, in their larval stage, use their large, sickle-shaped jaws to build steep-sided traps. When a careless ant

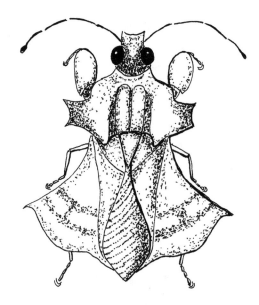

Ambush bug (Phynatidae family). Concealed by their body shape, color, and pattern, ambush bugs wait on goldenrod or other yellow flowers for a nectar-seeking insect to come along.

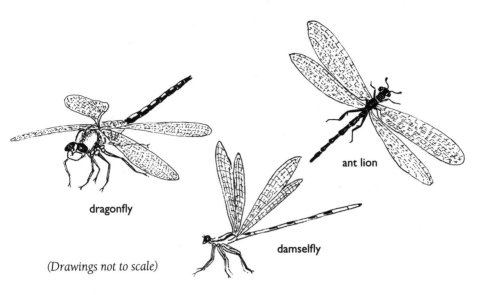

dragonfly

ant lion

damselfly

(Drawings not to scale)

or some other insect tumbles into the trap, it cannot get out, and dinner is served for the ant lion.

If you spend some time engaged in mantis watching, you will become aware that they are slow-moving, capable, and cunning insects that are formidable predators. Although mantises are harmless to humans, they eat a large variety of animals in addition to insects and spiders. In the tropical rain forests, a four-inch mantis was reported eating a ten-inch snake. Hummingbirds are another unlikely food source that yield to this formidable predator,

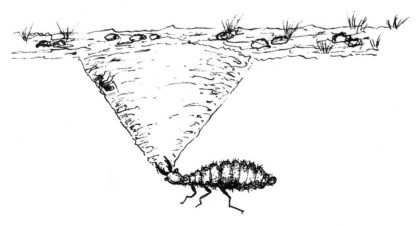

A larval stage ant lion, or doodlebug, waits at the bottom of its trap for a careless insect to tumble in.

as are small mice that may become trapped by the deadly claws. Even bats have made it onto the mantis menu.

If you have the opportunity to watch a mantis eat a few meals, you will notice that there is a fixed pattern to the process, regardless of the size of the prey. Once the prey is secure in its viselike grip, the mantis bites into the back of the prey's neck, severing the main ganglia. The struggle is over. It may take the mantis some time and a great deal of energy to position the prey so that the lethal bite can be made.

As summer wanes, mantises often experience extreme hunger, which they cannot satisfy as their ordinary insect prey are no longer readily available. In these difficult times, mantises have been known to eat their own legs.

Mantises are not without their enemies. Edwin Way Teal reports in *Circle of the Season* how he observed a blue jay hop toward a mantis. The mantis reared up and lashed out with its spiny forelegs at the approaching bird. The persistent blue jay kept trying to close in on the mantis. It tried several times from different angles. But the mantis was always poised with its deadly weapons ready to strike. Eventually the blue jay flew off, leaving the victorious mantis unharmed.

Praying mantises belong to the order Orthoptera. They share membership in this group with crickets, grasshoppers, cockroaches, and walking sticks. Members of the order have been divided, based on physical characteristics, into suborders, which are further divided into families. Mantises belong to the family Mantidae, walking sticks are members of the family Phasmatidae, and cockroaches are placed in the family Blattidae.

The eggs that produce mantises are laid in the autumn. Mating between male and female may take as long as twenty-four hours. Regardless of how long it takes, after mating, the female devours the male (see Chapter Note 1). About two or three weeks later, she produces a frothy substance in which she lays her eggs, about 150 of them. This hardens into a Styrofoamlike cover. Depending on the species, it can take as long as five hours to make a nest; some females make as many as twenty nests in their short lifetime. The egg cases with their tenants will overwinter attached to twigs and plant stems. Some have even been found on outdoor furniture. The egg cases are initially white, but as time passes, they become yellow and finally brown. With a short life span coded in their genes, all mantises that hatched in June will die by the time autumn becomes winter.

All is not peaceful for the developing larvae within an egg case. Although the egg case is hard and tough, it cannot always protect the eggs from the sharp teeth of a hungry mouse or a peck from a woodpecker's bill. But in spite of many different attempts to break into the case, most larvae survive until spring. If you are very lucky, you might find the walnut-sized egg case of a praying mantis secured to a twig while taking a winter walk.

As the weather becomes warmer, the balls of hardened froth grow soggy and spongy, and the hatchlings begin to emerge, encased in thin sheaths. They dangle head down, attached by fine threads to the nest and to the egg sac. During this time, they are vulnerable to a host of predators. With the help of powerful jaws, they soon tear themselves free from the sheaths and scatter in different directions to live solitary predaceous lives.

About thirty to forty minutes after leaving the nest, they become the color of their species. These young praying mantises are similar to the adults in behavior. They also resemble the adults in appearance, except that they lack wings.

The ravenous hatchlings feed on small flies and mosquitoes. If no food is available, however, they will eat each other. In a few weeks, they will add small caterpillars and small butterflies to their diet. The young are vulnerable to hungry frogs, toads, and lizards, but if they manage to live through the first week, they have a good chance of reaching maturity.

There are about twenty species of mantises in the United States and Canada. The Carolina mantis (*Stagmomantis carolina*) is native to the United States. Although it thrives in the South, it has traveled as far west as California. A smaller European mantis (*Mantis religiosa*) lives throughout most of the eastern states and in Canada, where it is now well established in Ontario. The oriental mantis (*Tenodera sinensis*) arrived here from China about seventy-five years ago and is widely distributed across the country. Today it is the most common mantis in the eastern United States.

THE WORLD OF PRAYING MANTISES

What you will need	Science skills
basic kit	*observing*
time	*comparing*
	recording

OBSERVATIONS

Finding and Capturing a Mantis. Mantises may be found from midsummer through October or November. If you are extremely lucky, you might find a mantis inside your house. Although they are sometimes found resting on a windowsill, screen door, or plant on the patio, usually mantises are discovered by accident in their natural environment.

It is relatively easy to capture these slow-moving insects. An insect net would be helpful but is not necessary because you can usually scoop the mantis up with your hands. Be gentle. The mantis will not bite you, but if you handle it roughly, you can expect to get a pinch from its powerful forelegs.

If you cannot find any mantises, you may be able to purchase them from an organic gardening store or biological supply house (see Chapter Note 2), although they may be available only at certain times of the year.

Mantis Anatomy. How would you describe the mantis? What are some of the unusual characteristics of this insect? Is it all one color? How does the front set of wings differ from the hind wings? Can you see a clearly defined head, thorax, and abdomen? Three pairs of legs? In what ways are the legs similar or different? Describe the eyes. Are they located in the front or on each side of the head?

Mantis Behavior. Hold the mantis in your hand with an open palm and let it explore. Allow the slow-moving mantis to climb where it will on your

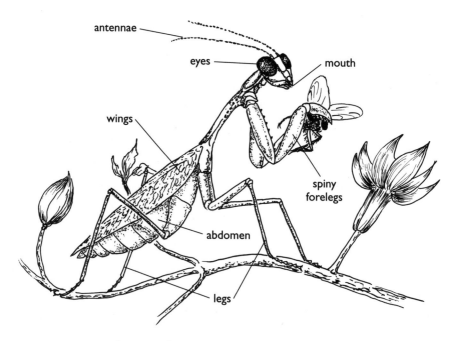

Anatomy of a praying mantis (Mantidae family)

THE ANIMALS

extended arm. Does it try to climb on your shoulder? Your head? Keep a record of its behavior throughout its exploration.

Although it is doubtful that a mantis will learn to recognize you, it will become accustomed to being handled by you. Habituation is the simplest form of learning and is often seen in insects. When becoming habituated, an insect learns to ignore or become less responsive to a stimulus that it repeatedly experiences. For example, workers in an ant colony will initially attack a glass rod poked into the nest. Scientists discovered that if the disturbance is repeated frequently, the ants gradually become less responsive to it. Many insects, praying mantises among them, become habituated to frequent handling and can thus be "tamed."

The mantis has a particular way of cleaning itself. Watch how it does it, and record your observations. After you have seen the process a few times, what generalizations can you make about the grooming habits of mantises?

Mantis Territory. One observer recorded a mantis perched for several days on a potted plant. During that time, it moved only a few inches from the place it was originally seen. Have you had a similar experience? Was it always the same mantis? How can you tell? To guarantee that the mantis you see on successive days is not a different one, capture the mantis and put a tiny dab of paint on its abdomen with a fine paintbrush. If you have more than one mantis put a mark of a different color on each so you can distinguish them. Make a map of the location of the mantis when you first observed it. For the next several days, record its movements. What did you discover?

You can safely let the mantis roam around your house, provided you don't have any predators living there, such as a cat or dog. Mantises find curtains, chairs, lamps, and other places to be satisfactory perches. Houseplants are particularly desirable. Does it seem to prefer some perches better than others? How long does it remain in any one place?

EXPLORATIONS

Mantises as Pets. Mantises are more helpful when left outside, where they will eat plant-eating insects, but if you want to explore mantis behavior more closely, you can keep one as a pet. Mantis needs are minimal, although they must be fed live insects. They do not move around much, so they don't need a great deal of space. A clear plastic container with a lid makes a satisfactory cage, but be sure to make ventilation holes in the lid. A fish tank will work as well, but you will need a cover. You can make an adequate lid by attaching wire mesh to a frame that fits securely on the tank. Gallon glass jars, although adequate for many other types of insects, are not suitable for a mantis, because the diameter of the jar is not large enough to allow the insect to move about freely. You can always purchase a container from a pet store that you can keep for observing other small animals.

Do not line the bottom of the cage with sand, soil, or any other covering, because the insects you provide for food will find that an effective hiding place. Add a sturdy plant stem with some green leaves for the mantis to use as a perch. Two twigs are usually enough; the mantis can get tangled in the plant material if you add too much to the container.

Observe the mantis for several days. How many times did you see the mantis on the plant? On the lid? If you have added twigs from different plants, which kind does the mantis seem to prefer for a perch? Or does it prefer to hang on to the lid rather than the twigs you provided? Keep a record of your observations.

Providing Food and Water. Mantises are ravenous eaters and particularly enjoy grasshoppers, moths, flies, crickets, and katydids. If available, they will also eat yellow jackets that happen to fly within their reach. One way to secure food for your mantis is to set up an insect trap. Put some raw meat in the bottom of a jar, and insert a funnel into the mouth. The funnel should fit into the mouth of the jar but not drop into it. Leave the jar outdoors. Among the insects your trap will attract are flies and beetles.

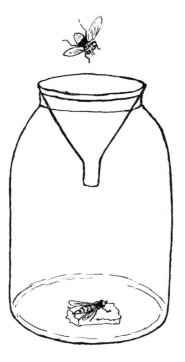

A jar with raw meat at the bottom and a funnel in its open mouth will make an easy and effective insect trap.

During the fall, you can easily collect field crickets. Look for them in leaf litter and other damp places, such as piles of grass cuttings. Frequently they will find their way into your house. Their chirping will help you identify their location. Crickets are easy to trap with your hands, but their glossy coating makes them slippery. A medium-sized jar also works well. Pop the jar over the cricket, and slip your hand or a three-by-five index card over the mouth of the jar. Since you will need more than one cricket, keep a larger jar on hand for your captives.

Try feeding your mantis some other kinds of live insects. If you are unable to trap any insects, a pet store may be able to supply you with fruit flies.

Design an investigation to determine the mantis's preferred food. Is it crickets? Fruit flies? Moths? Flies? Some other insect? You need to offer food samples several times before you can make a statement about which the mantis prefers. Watch the mantis eat a few meals. Record the process in your notebook. Does there appear to be a pattern to it? How can you tell when you have introduced an undesirable food? How long does it take for the mantis to eat various insects? Add several crickets to the mantis cage. How many does the mantis eat in one hour? Two hours? Keep a record of foods eaten and foods not eaten in a chart similar to the one below. Rank the foods in order of observed preferences.

FOOD CHOICE

Date	Type of Food	Eaten	Not Eaten

A pet mantis also needs water. You can supply this by spraying the sides of the container. One investigator reported feeding a mantis milk with an eye dropper. Can you train your mantis to drink water from an eye dropper? Keep a log of what you did and how the mantis responded. How long did it take for the mantis to learn to take water from the eye dropper?

Mantis Defense Posture. When frightened, a mantis will assume a menacing stance. It achieves this by opening its wings and drawing back its upper body before striking a prey or intruder into its territory. Move your hand suddenly, palm open, toward a mantis as if you were going to hit it. What does it do? Does it strike at your hand or simply try to nudge it out of the way? Is the movement similar to or different from the rocking movement a mantis makes just before it strikes a meal?

Mating. If you put male and female mantises of the same species together, they will usually mate within a few days during late summer or fall. The male mantis is eaten by the female after mating, although sometimes he is devoured during the mating act, which can last for several hours. Sometime after the female lays her eggs, she ceases eating. Shortly thereafter, she dies.

If the female left the frothy blobs that contain her eggs on the twigs in the cage, you need to put them outdoors until they hatch in the early spring. Left indoors, they will hatch during the winter, and unless you have prepared for the hatchlings' arrival, there will be no food for them.

Hatching Mantis Eggs. If your mantis has not laid any eggs, look for frothy masses with wiggly seams firmly attached to the stems of tough weeds, grasses, or bare twigs that seem to be strong enough to withstand the winds of winter. Mantises prefer to leave egg cases on goldenrod, bayberry, privet, sumac, honeysuckle, and, to a lesser extent, grass stems. The size and shape of the egg cases vary with the species of mantis. If you find an egg case outdoors, leave it attached to a piece of the vegetation. If you cannot find any egg cases, you can order them from a biological supply house (see Chapter Note 2).

You'll need an empty gallon jar—the kind that holds mayonnaise, pickles, or relish. One can be had by asking at a delicatessen. Wash it thoroughly. Put the egg case, along with the piece of vegetation to which it is attached, in the jar. Cover the jar with a piece of nylon or cotton, and secure it with a rubber

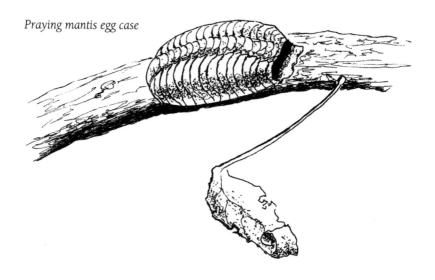

Praying mantis egg case

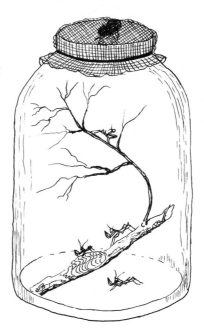

This would be a good setup to house your praying mantis egg mass and the young that will emerge from it.

band. Cut a cross in the cover, put a cotton plug in the hole, and wet it. This will be the mantises' water supply, so you need to keep the cotton moist.

When do the eggs begin to hatch? How many young mantises are there? If they are very active and counting them is difficult, you can put the jar into the refrigerator for about five minutes. The cool temperature will slow them down. How long does it take for their wings to become functional?

Mantises will only eat live insects, so unless you can cultivate a supply of fruit flies for the baby mantises, you will have to release them outdoors. If they remain together without live food, they will eat each other.

CHAPTER NOTES

1. Will a female mantis mate and dine on other males after she has already mated and fed on one male? This interesting question was answered long ago. A French naturalist who lived in the same era as Charles Darwin decided to find out. He introduced a succession of six male mantises into a cage with a female that had already mated and dined on her mate. To his amazement, the female proceeded to mate with and feed on all of the introduced males.

2.   One biological supply house from which you can obtain praying mantises or mantis eggs is Carolina Biological Supply, 2700 York Rd., Burlington, NC 27215, (336) 584-0381, www.carolina.com.

CHAPTER 6

Ants

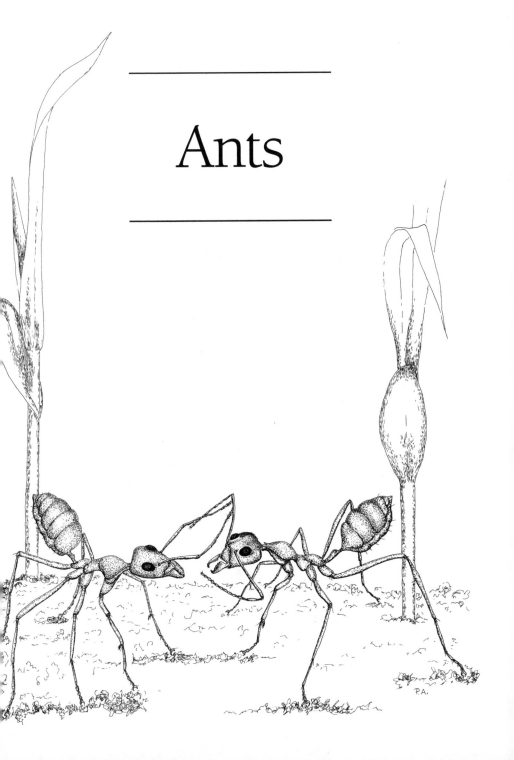

INDUSTRIOUS TUNNELERS

About ninety-five hundred known species of ants inhabit the world, and they belong to three hundred genera. When the myrmecologists, scientists who study ants, finish identifying all the species, it is believed that there may be as many as fifteen thousand, which leaves five thousand to six thousand species still unknown. If these newly discovered ants follow the established pattern, most of them will be found in the tropics.

With numbers like these, it's hard to imagine that there is anyone who doesn't know an ant when he or she sees one, but what most people may not know is how these quick-moving creatures are woven into the tapestry of living things.

Ants have been around for a long time. About 200 million years ago, during the Triassic period, one of the first insect orders, Hymenoptera, composed of bees, wasps, and ants, began to evolve. The first ants are believed to have developed from nonsocial wasps. The oldest known ants appeared about 90 million years ago and were contemporaries of the dinosaurs. Scientists know about these early ants because they have found many of them perfectly preserved in a fossilized resin called amber. When this sticky resin oozed from plants millions of years ago, as it still does today, insects frequently got stuck in it and were covered and preserved. Over time, the resin got rock hard. Amber is treasured as a gemstone for rings, necklaces, and bracelets, and people search for this translucent stone, with its golden glow.

Insects trapped in amber can be as old as the earliest resin-producing plants, which were probably seed ferns that existed about 360 million years ago. The most frequently studied amber is a mere 25 to 130 million years old, as amber from earlier times is usually too fragmented to be of value. From these insects, scientists learn which species were living during a given period and where they thrived, including such places as the Dominican Republic, Mexico, Canada, the Baltic, and China.

In 1967, while rock hunting in New Jersey, a pair of hobbyists found encased in amber what scientists call "wasp-ant," the missing piece in ant evolution that connected some modern ants and nonsocial wasps. These ant remains dated to the late Cretaceous age, about 80 million years ago. On close examination, the specimen resembled modern ants. The thorax was reduced in size, and it had a pinched-down waist, or pedicel, where it joined the rest of the abdomen, just like today's ants. The mandibles looked like those of wasps, it had a protruding stinger, and its antennae had features of those of both ants and wasps, but it lacked wings. Perhaps the most important characteristic was the presence of the antibiotic-secreting metaplural gland, which is the key

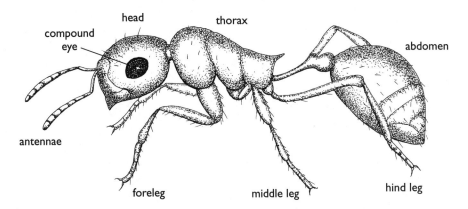

The external structure of a typical ant (Formicidae family) clearly shows the waist between the thorax and the abdomen.

diagnostic trait of modern ants. The secretions from this gland allow ants to keep their nests free of parasitic invaders. It appears that the presence of this gland and its secretions, along with the ants' social habits, were responsible for the evolutionary success of ants. Edward O. Wilson and William L. Brown, two renowned field biologists, identified this extinct specimen as part of the ancient and previously unknown ant subfamily Sphecomyrminae, which means "wasp-ant." The discovery was named *Sphecomyrma freyi* to honor the couple who found the ant in amber, a Mr. and Mrs. Frey.

Other ant species that lived millions of years ago were found by scientists in what is called Dominican amber. Identical ants are still seen today, and they have migrated from the West Indies to North and South America.

Although we don't see the ants invading our homes wearing wings, fertile males have two pairs of wings that lift them into the air during the brief mating flight with a winged queen. The leading pair of the smaller hindwings is equipped with a row of hooks that fit onto a pair of hooks on the trailing edge of the forewings. This arrangement also is found in wasps and bees. As ants started evolving from wasps, they took up residence in the soil and wings became more of a hindrance than a help. The result was that most ants lost them.

Ants belong to the Formicidae family, and although they live in diverse habitats, the warm, moist tropics are especially to their liking. This is evident by the findings of dedicated scientists who spend much of their time in those latitudes searching for new information about these highly successful insects. For example, Wilson and his team identified forty-three species of ants living on a single tree found on a preserve in Peru. This is more than the total

Life cycle of an ant

1. Egg

2. Larva

3. Pupa enclosed in a cocoon

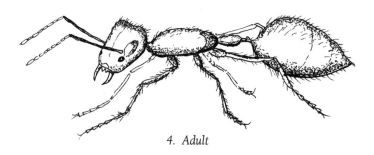

4. Adult

number of species found in the British Isles. This extreme reduction in the number of ant species as you travel north is typical. As the distance from the equator continues to increase, there is a corresponding decrease in the number of ant species. There are only three known ant species thriving above the tree line in the Arctic. The same pattern exists as the distance from the equator increases to the south, but there are no known species of ants in Antarctica.

As with all Hymenoptera, ants develop through four stages of complete metamorphosis: egg, larva, pupa, and adult. The length of these stages varies with the species.

Life for ants begins in eggs, which are produced by a fertile queen. These extremely small eggs are easily missed by the casual observer. They are guarded and cared for by sterile female workers in the nest. One of the specific jobs the workers have is to keep the eggs free of fungal growth, which they do by licking them.

When the larvae emerge from the eggs, they enter the second stage of their life cycle. Like the larvae of all insects, their main goal is to eat and grow. The job of the workers during the developmental stages is to care for the young, which includes feeding, cleaning, and protecting them from harm. The undeveloped ants are dependent on the workers for their every need. They are also subject to the whims of environmental factors such as temperature and humidity. The duration of each developmental stage depends on the species. At the appropriate time, which is genetically determined, the larvae enter the pupal phase of their development. When they emerge from this phase, they are adult ants with certain responsibilities to the colony.

While the development of the young ants is progressing, the queen of the colony continues to lay more eggs. This is her sole job throughout life. She is an "egg-producing machine" until she dies.

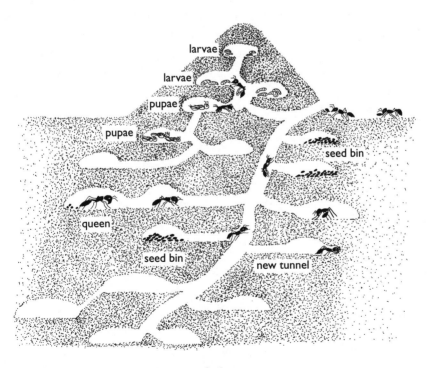

Cross section of a harvester ant nest

When a colony of ants reaches a certain degree of stability, it generates chemicals that signal the existing queen or queens (there may be more than one queen in a colony) to produce unfertilized eggs that will develop into new winged queens and winged males. When the right time arrives, these fertile ants will leave the nest at the same time as sexual ants of the same species from other nearby nests, so that in a given area there may be hundreds of thousands of ants taking flight simultaneously. The swarms of ants may rise to such heights that we are unable to see them, but reports tell us that "spectacular" is an understatement for this high-flying behavior.

This annual ritual causes great excitement among the worker ants. They can be seen outside the nest running here and there, with no apparent goal except to be part of this great moment in the life of the colony.

The males die after mating, but the queens seek a place to begin a new colony. Sometimes they will enter an established colony of their own species or of an alien species. In this case, her offspring will be either permanent or temporary parasites.

Following this highly ritualized mating process, the queens remove their wings either by biting them off or by rubbing them against a solid object, such as a rock or tree bark. They then search for a suitable nest site, which varies according to the species, although you have probably seen them in the soil under stones and between cracks in the sidewalk. The nest can be very simple, with only a small number of ants populating it, or it can be a complex maze of tunnels and galleries with thousands of ants in residence. The "rooms" become pantries for food and places for the eggs and developing larvae and pupae. Some of these nests are shallow, but others extend several feet below the ground. The mound-building ants spend the warmer months above-ground, but when cold weather arrives, they retreat below the frost line. Queens of some species begin colonies in such odd sites as galls, acorns, and plant stems, or behind tree bark. The life span of queens varies with the species. The queens of leaf-cutter ants live as long as fifteen to twenty years, but those of army ants live only about five years.

The first eggs laid by the new queen develop into infertile, wingless female workers. Their job is to gather food and feed the queen, which is usually about twice the size of the largest worker. In return for these efforts, the queen feeds the workers eggs and regurgitated food. Subsequent broods are also cared for by the workers. The life of the colony is their responsibility. The youngest workers are nurses that care for the eggs, larvae, and pupae. They spend most of their time moving the young from one part of the nest to another, depending on conditions of temperature and humidity that are best for the young. In feeding the larvae, they receive a sweet substance for their effort.

If an ant nest is disturbed, the ants scurry around frantically, and you may see some ants carrying white objects in their mouths. These are not eggs, but helpless larvae and pupae that would die if the workers did not rush to their aid.

The workers are also responsible for cleaning the nest, burying the dead, and defending the nest from intruders. As the colony increases in numbers, the workers build additional galleries and tunnels. There is no aggression among members of the colony. The jobs are carried out without any fuss. It is because of this that ant colonies are often referred to as a superorganism—a unit that functions as a single entity. Each ant is comparable to a cell in an organism.

Ant colonies are caste or class societies wherein each individual has a clearly defined role. Some colonies have specialists such as soldier ants, which are larger than workers and have heavier mandibles. Leaf-cutter ants have specialized tiny workers whose job it is to ride shotgun on leaf segments to protect the average-sized workers, which carry the leaves, from parasitic flies that try to deposit their eggs on the heads of the carrier ants.

The main organizers of life in the ant colony are chemicals. Chemicals released within the colony cause the workers to respond and maintain cooperative and altruistic behavior. One ant left alone would not be able to survive. Communication between ants is accomplished by passing odors via glandular secretions from one ant to another. These chemical secretions combine with environmental factors, such as the nesting material, to give each colony's nest a characteristic odor of its own. This enables ants to recognize their own nest, as well as an intruder whose odor is not familiar. We are unable to detect most of these odors, but scientists tell us some ants have odors that resemble such things as tobacco juice, the oil of bitter almonds, potato blossoms, smoke, rotten coconuts, and rancid butter, to name a few. It is the ants' antennae that are sensitive to these chemicals. If an ant should lose an antenna, it becomes severely handicapped and will not live very long after the loss.

The exchange of food, or mutual feeding, is another behavior that holds the community together. When ants in a colony meet each other throughout the day, they will stop, feel each other with their antennae, and pass a drop of special food from one to the other. The antennae are specially designed structures in which each segment controls a different aspect of the ant's life. One

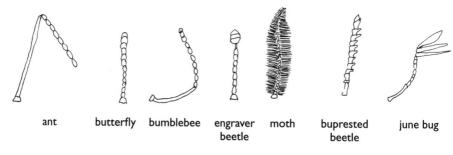

| ant | butterfly | bumblebee | engraver beetle | moth | buprested beetle | june bug |

Some examples of insect antennae

segment of an antenna detects nest odor and helps prevent the ant from entering a colony that is not its own. Another part tells the ant if another is a descendant of the same or a different queen. Still another segment detects odor that the ant itself left as it walked a trail, allowing the ant to follow its own trail back to the colony. Another part tells a worker what is needed by a developing ant. The antennae also help the ants identify unknown objects through their size and shape.

Although the ants' antennae are their primary organs for learning about their environment, ants also have compound eyes. On close examination, each eye looks like a mosaic of hexagonal facets that are grouped together in a single structure. Each facet contains a separate lens and a light-sensitive cell, and each contributes a part of the whole picture. Generally, sight in ants is not acute, although some ants, such as the workers and soldiers of the leaf-cutting group, have large compound eyes and will respond to the movement of an object an inch from their heads. Other species of ants are totally blind.

Ants also find their way by orienting themselves to polarized light from the sun. They can travel toward or away from the light source and can move at an angle to the light stimulus. Researchers tell us ants can also compensate for the movement of the sun.

There is a great deal more to learn about ants. Many interesting books are available for people who are interested in finding out more about these fascinating creatures. Ant societies are sometimes compared to our human societies. They have a class culture. They have battles with ants from different colonies. Their colonies resemble factory assembly lines. Workers, soldiers, nurses, harmonious cooperation, communication, and mating rituals seem to make up a world that is very similar to our own. However, ants greatly outnumber humans, and they have been around for much longer than we have. Perhaps we can learn some things from them on how to live in harmony with our planet.

Caution: When handling ants, it's a good idea to wear some kind of hand protection. A pair of padded tweezers will help you pick up ants without injuring them.

OBSERVATIONS

When and Where to Look for Ants. Ask any homeowner, and he or she will tell you that ants are found throughout the year. They are most obvious during the spring, however, when they are enlarging an established home or excavating for new nests. During this time, you may see ants from different colonies involved in territorial battles and doing other fascinating things, such as following trails, foraging, cleaning themselves, and feeding one another.

Summer is the time of greatest activity, although some become less active and retreat to the cool of their nests during August's heat. During the decline of temperatures in September and October, ants become sluggish and eventually snuggle into their nests for the winter. During this time, they do not eat, and unlike their cousins the bees, they do not manufacture body heat.

Ants can appear in a variety of places. Look for them in rotting logs in woodpiles, in small earth mounds that you find in your backyard, or in cracks in a cement driveway or walkway. Of course, the best way to find ants is to have a picnic.

Make a note of the different places in which you find ants. Include the time of year when you discovered them.

Ant Anatomy. The ant has three main body parts, which identify it as an insect: head, thorax, and abdomen. The head is connected to the thorax by a thin "neck," which is often difficult to see. The thorax is connected to the abdomen by a stemlike pedicel, or waist. This abdominal stalk has one segment in some ants and two in others. Each of the segments has a bump. In primitive species, such as fire ants and harvester ants (subfamily Myrmicinae), there are two of these bumps; in more advanced species such as carpenter ants and field ants (subfamily Formicinae), there is only one. With the help of a hand lens, observe an ant. Make a drawing of it, identifying the major body parts that distinguish it as an insect. Can you see the bumps? How many are there?

The ant's antennae are long, and the bend, or elbow, between the first and second segments is characteristic of ants. The number of segments in each antenna ranges from five to thirteen, and each controls a different aspect of the ant's life. Compare the ant antennae with those of members of the Lepidoptera order, such as butterflies and moths. How do they differ?

Ant Interactions. The experts who have studied worker ants tell us there are several levels of interactions between them. If you spend time watching the activity around an ant nest, you may be able to observe these behaviors. In one of these interactions, one ant directs the tips of its antennae over the surface of another ant. In a closer interaction, called licking, one ant touches its mouth to the body of the other ant. The ant being licked often becomes still while this is going on.

Other interactions are associated with aggression. These occur when members of different colonies, of the same or different species, meet. In an aggressive mode, one ant grabs a section of the body of the other ant with its mandibles and drags it away. If you move an ant from one colony to another, you might be able to set up one of these aggressive behaviors.

How many of these interactions can you observe? Describe them in your notebook.

Varieties of Ants. Scientists have organized this very large family of insects (Formicidae) into subfamilies based on physical characteristics, behaviors, habitats, and the types of nests they build.

Subfamily Myrmicinae. This is the largest subfamily of ants, with about three hundred species illustrating diverse habitats and habits. Some Myrmicinae are fungus growers, others are carnivorous, and still others are parasitic. Some live in large colonies, and others thrive with only a few dozen nest mates. All Myrmicinae have a second division of the pedicel, an addition that allows greater flexibility of the gaster (the enlarged part of the abdomen behind the pedicel), which in turn improves the efficiency of the stinger. Some of the more familiar are listed below.

Harvester ants (**Pogonomyrmex *sp.* and Pheidole *sp.*).** These ants live in fields and farms, where their primary food is seeds. They also feed on termites and other insects, fruits, berries, and flowers. Chewing the inner portion of the seeds and mixing it with saliva produces a sticky substance, which the ant stores in its crop. The mix can be digested by the ant or passed on to other

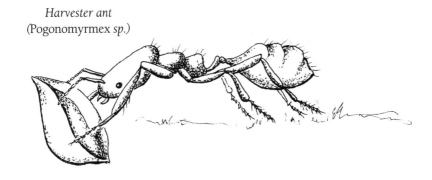

Harvester ant
(Pogonomyrmex *sp.*)

ants in the colony. They are also known to store seeds in their nests. The nests of harvester ants are in the ground, but the entrances to these nests are easily seen. Surrounding the entrance, you frequently will find a crater rather than a mound. This is a good identification clue for your search. Some harvester ants are soldiers with large mandibles; their job is to defend the colony. If you make a disturbance at the nest entrance, you may observe the soldiers emerging to do their job. Various numbers have been given for the population of harvest ant colonies, ranging from fifty thousand to ninety thousand.

Fungus-growing ants (Trachymyrmex *sp.*). These ants feed on fungi, simple plants that lack chlorophyll, which they grow in the nest.

Leaf-cutting ants (Atta *sp.*). These ants feed on fungi grown on pieces of leaves the ants bring into the colony. The relationship between the ants and their fungus farms is called symbiosis, a term used to describe organisms of different species living together in a mutually beneficial arrangement. The ants use a mulch made of insect excrement, especially from caterpillars. The first brood produced by the queen consists of the smallest workers, called

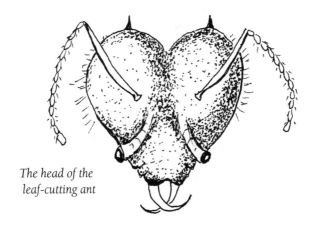

The head of the leaf-cutting ant

minims. They initially leave the nest to cut and bring back leaves, but as other, larger workers are produced, these tiny workers are assigned to spend the rest of their lives in the darkness of their huge nest. These ants are generally found in the tropics of Central and South America, but there are some living in the U.S. Southwest. They have arrowhead-shaped heads and prongs on their backs. It's an interesting sight to see them marching in characteristic single file back to the nest, as each member carries a small piece of leaf taken from plants in the area.

Fire ants (Solenopsis sp.). Two fire ant species were accidentally brought into Alabama from South America in 1918. These ants are most troublesome, due to their aggressive nature and the ferocious sting they can inflict. Their sting has been known to kill birds and small mammals. The ant attacks by pinching the victim's skin with its jaws while jabbing with a stinger located at the end of its abdomen—a one-two punch.

• Red fire ant (*Solenopsis invicta*). This species is the more common of the two and is found in abundance in the southeastern United States, from the Carolinas to Texas.

• Black fire ant (*Solenopsis richteri*). This species is found in only a few southeastern states. Their nests are mounds, usually hard-crusted, that may be as high and wide as a meter and contain as many as a hundred thousand individual ants. Fields, farms, yards, and recreational areas such as ball fields are preferred home sites. There may be as many as a hundred nests per acre, and these nests sometimes damage farm machinery. The antennae of these ants have ten segments, unlike others in the subfamily. Be cautious if you get close enough to observe these segments.

Subfamily Formicinae. This second-largest subfamily of ants claims about two hundred species and is more widely distributed than the Myrmicinae. Formicinae do not sting, but their bite can be unpleasant, especially if they garnish it with a squirt of formic acid—another one-two punch.

Fire ant
(Solenopsis *sp.*)

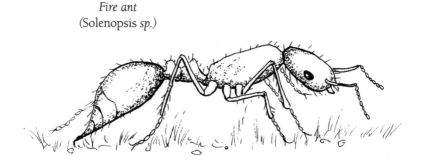

THE ANIMALS

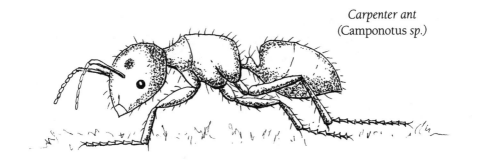

Carpenter ant
(Camponotus *sp.*)

Carpenter ants (Camponotus *sp.*). This group holds some of the largest ants in North America. They live throughout the East and are also seen west to Texas. You can find them practically everywhere in North America where it is not too cold. They make their nests in dead and dying trees, stumps, logs, and even in frames of houses and other wooden buildings. They feed on dead and living insects. A nest might have twenty-five hundred workers, a few males, and a single queen. One species, *Camponotus pennsylvanicus,* chews wood to make its nest, but unlike termites, carpenter ants do not feed on wood. They love sweets of all kinds. Look for carpenter ants wherever there is dead wood.

Slave-maker ants (Polyergus *sp.*). Sometimes called Amazon ants, these ants are particularly noted for their sickle-shaped mandibles, which effectively puncture the heads of their adversaries. However, these weapons are useless for carrying the queen's eggs or feeding the young. This handicap makes them totally dependent on slaves throughout the life of the colony. When a new queen starts a colony, she raids the nest of another *Polyergus* species and kills the reigning queen. With their queen gone, the workers of the raided colony adopt the Amazon queen as their own, giving service to her by caring for her eggs and young. A brilliant red species *(Polyergus lucidus)* is fairly common in the eastern part of the United States.

Amazon/slave-maker ants
(Polyergus *sp.*)

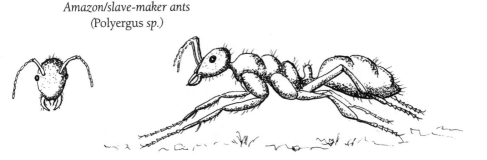

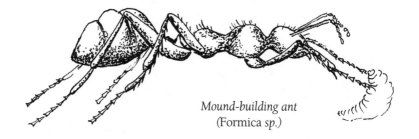

Mound-building ant
(Formica *sp.*)

Mound-building ants (Formica *sp.*). These ants are common throughout the eastern part of the United States. *Formica pallide-fulva* is found in mounds built in the soil. Their nests are made from earth and plant material, such as decaying leaves and grasses, and are about two to three feet high and one to two feet wide. You will find these nests in clearings in the woods of the mountains of the eastern states. This species of mound-building ants is noted for capturing pupae of the timid common brown formica ant *(Formica fusca subsericea)* and using them as slaves when they emerge from their pupal phase.

Red and black slave-making ants (Formica sanguinea). These ants are found throughout the United States. They live in brush. In the West, they find sagebrush to their liking. They form armies that march into the territory of the same timid *Formica fusca,* overwhelming these lesser ants and capturing their larvae and pupae. The emerging adults are turned into slaves.

Ants versus Termites. Termites are frequently called white ants, but they have a caste system that is more highly developed than the class system of ants, bees, or wasps. Their society is made up of fertile males and females. Some have wings, and others lack fully developed wings. There are also soldier termites in the nest. Termites can be found in decaying wood, such as rotting logs and dead or dying trees. Capture one of them and compare it with ants. How are they similar? Different? (See Chapter Note 1.)

Carpenter ants may be confused with termites. It's not unusual to see these large black ants entering or leaving a dead tree or log in an almost steady procession. If you see this happening, break off some bark and open it. You will find tunnels forming a rather complicated series of parallel chambers, which in an old nest become a labyrinth of galleries, halls, and rooms. The tunnels of termites run parallel to one another, usually with the grain of the wood, but they do not form such an intricate series of tunnels and chambers as those found in the nests of carpenter ants. Termite galleries are formed from a grayish, mortarlike material composed of excrement that the termites make.

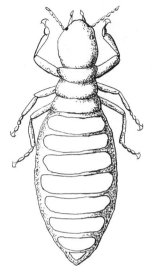

*Worker termite
(order Isoptera)*

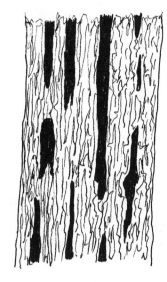

Galleries of termites

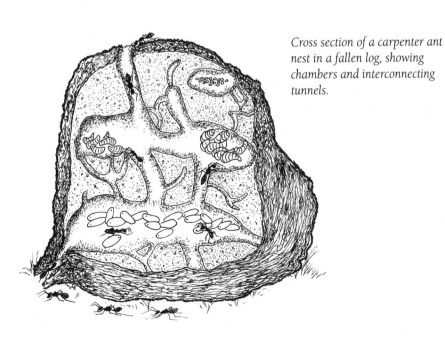

*Cross section of a carpenter ant
nest in a fallen log, showing
chambers and interconnecting
tunnels.*

The queen ant, the only fertile ant, may boast a thousand times the body weight of a minor worker.

Other Comparisons. Compare an ant from the colony with the queen. How are they similar? Different?

Next, compare other insects you find, such as a moth, a ladybug, and a daddy longlegs, with each other and with an ant. How do they differ? What do they have in common? Draw a picture of each, illustrating the similarities and differences.

Grooming. The antennae of ants are very important to the survival of the individual and to the colony as well. Personal grooming removes dirt and other debris from the antennae and the rest of the ant's body.

If you have a large ant and a high-powered lens, you may be able to see the ant's cleaning tools, comblike hairs in the midsection of each leg. Write a description of them. How do these leg segments differ from the others?

Since ants spend a good bit of time cleaning themselves throughout the day, you will have an opportunity to see the process. This is a fascinating event to watch. The ant cleans its antennae by pulling each one through the "comb" and removing the collected dirt with its mouth. The third pair of legs is cleaned by the second pair, which is cleaned by the combs of the first pair. How is the first pair cleaned?

Large Groups of Ants. Sometimes you will see large groups of ants swarming on the grass or pavement. Frequently mistaken for termites, they are winged males and females emerging from nests to mate. Look for their discarded wings lying on the ground.

At other times you may see large groups of ants of two different sizes engaged in aggressive behavior. These ants are probably from two different colonies and are at war over the location of nest sites. What is the outcome of the battle? Where do the different groups of ants go?

EXPLORATIONS

Collecting Ants. The best time to look for ants is from the late spring into autumn. You will need a shallow empty can, some honey, gloves, tongs or padded tweezers, and a Ziploc bag. Put some honey in the can and leave it outside on the ground. How long does it take for ants to find your sweet bait? When ants are swarming over the can, put on the gloves, pick up the ants with the tongs or tweezers, and place them in the plastic bag.

Another method is to dig for ants. Look for a telltale ant mound in your yard. Wearing gloves, use a garden trowel to dig into the nest. Empty the contents of your trowel onto a light-colored cloth placed on the ground near the mound, and any ants in the debris will be easily seen. To find the queen, dig deeper. Pick up the ants with tongs or padded tweezers, put them in a jar, and secure it with a lid. Put the queen in a separate container. Don't forget to put air holes in the lids.

The ants will be very active; you can slow them down by placing the sealed bag or jar in the refrigerator for twenty minutes or so. All insects respond to the temperature of the air around them. They do not have the internal controls that mammals have.

Ant Trails. Ants use different strategies to find their way back to their colony. A prominent part of the landscape, such as a rock, and the polarized light of the sun are helpful visual clues for the wandering ant, but the most common strategy is a scent trail on the ground marked by pheromones that the ant secretes.

You may safely work through this exploration with any ant except fire ants. When working with any ants, it's still a good idea to wear gloves, as any ant may bite. This exploration is best done from late spring into autumn, as this is the time when you can expect to find ant colonies. Look around your yard, driveway, and sidewalk for a colony of ants.

If you see ants following one another outside the nest, all going along the same path, rub your finger across the path. What happens to the parading ants? How do the ants coming along on the path behave? Do they get back on the trail? How long does it take for successive ants to restore the path? Do they have to find the food source first?

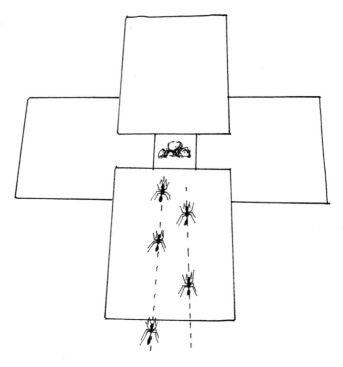

This setup will help you study ant scent trails.

Put a teaspoonful of honey or syrup about three feet away from the nest, and place four pieces of cardboard around it so that any trail over the cardboard will lead the ants to the honey. Watch the ants as they move from one place to another. Is their path a straight line? How do they use their antennae to follow the scent trail (a chemical path) laid down by the first ants that found the food? Wait until there are about thirty to forty ants traveling to and from the nest. Now turn the cardboard that is closest to the nest forty-five degrees from the sweet. What happens? Next turn the cardboard 180 degrees from the original position. What do the ants do? How do ants new to the trail behave? Record their behaviors in your notebook. Try this with other ants in other locations. Compare your results. What did you find out? (See Chapter Note 2.)

Foraging. If a find of food is too large, such as a dead insect, the ant goes back to the nest to find more workers to help bring the item back. It is fascinating to see the number of ants cooperating to bring a caterpillar, dead cricket, or bread crust back to the nest. One observer noticed that ants get better at pulling their prey over a period of about ten minutes, at which point they are pulling it at their maximum rate. The ants may pull in opposing directions for a while, but then they become efficient and begin to pull together in the same direction. A few common ant species do not drag large prey, but carry it back to the nest in little bits that they have torn off. Set a large food item such as a bread crust or dead insect near a colony and observe the ants' behavior. Do they carry it whole or tear off pieces? How long does it take for the ants to work as a team?

Do Ants Have Food Preferences? Place a variety of foods, such as honey, butter, jam, yogurt, water, milk, and small pieces of various fruits and vegetables, on a flat surface outdoors. Check the feeding station every thirty minutes or so. Do the ants appear to prefer certain foods? Try this investigation at several other places. Are your results similar or different?

Ant Farm. An ant farm is an excellent way to observe ants living in their nest. You can buy a kit from a toy store, pet store, nature or science store, or by contacting Uncle Milton, Giant Ant Farm, Culver City, CA 90232, www.unclemilton.com. A handbook is included.

An alternative to the commercial ant farm is to build your own. Instructions are available for building many different kinds of ant farms, and most of them are equally satisfactory. If you would like to build your own ant farm, you can find directions in the book *175 Amazing Nature Experiments,* by Rosie Harlow and Gareth Morgan (New York: Random House, 1991).

CHAPTER NOTES

1. Termites are soft-bodied and lack the ant's waist, and their antennae are straight and not angled like the ant's. Termites have very small eyes or no eyes at all, whereas ants have large, well-developed eyes. The heads of soldier termites are large and equipped with formidable jaws suited for chewing many different types of wood. Two species of termites live in the United States: *Reticulitermes flavipes* makes its home in the East, and *R. hesperus* is found throughout the West. An extinct species was recovered from Dominican amber, which dates their existence as far back as 30 to 40 million years.

2. Source: H. Steven Dashefsky, *Insect Biology: 49 Science Fair Projects* (New York: Tab Books, McGraw Hill, 1992), 35-37.

CHAPTER 7

Ladybugs

LOVABLE INSECTS

People like ladybugs. In hardware stores and garden centers, you will find artistic renditions of ladybugs designed to decorate your garden. If you go to any bookstore, you are guaranteed to find at least one delightfully illustrated children's book featuring ladybugs. Craft and gift shops are filled with ladybug creations. From sweatshirts to lamps, from jewelry to potholders, ladybugs reign supreme.

These lovable insects have a few different common names, which may cause some confusion. In some places they are called ladybird beetles, while elsewhere people know them as lady beetles, but people in the United States usually just call them ladybugs.

Ladybugs have six legs and three body parts (head, thorax, and abdomen), and scientists agree that they are insects. Within that classification, however, ladybugs are not grouped with the "true bugs." The true bug order, Hemiptera, includes such insects as assassin bugs and giant water bugs. Ladybugs belong to the group of insects called beetles, the order Coleoptera. Many other beetles are well known, such as Japanese beetles, weevils, and fireflies, but none shares the popularity of the ladybug. It may surprise you to know that there are more than 350,000 beetle species worldwide. This number is about 40 percent of all insect species. Even more surprising, there are more than 5,000 species of ladybugs around the world, and 370 of those species live in North America.

Known for hundreds of years for their huge appetite for harmful insects, the ladybug has been bestowed with supernatural powers in folklore. People once thought ladybugs could foretell good weather and a bountiful harvest. Many believed that ladybugs would bestow good luck on those who discovered them. The "lady" in ladybug refers to Our Lady, the Virgin Mary.

Ladybugs are the most voracious predators in our arsenal against plant pests, and they also pollinate flowers as they travel from plant to plant. These insects have an interesting history in the United States. Since colonial times, they have been known for their ability to destroy the insect pests that damage agricultural crops. But it was not until the late 1800s that this ability was utilized on a large scale in the United States. At that time, a pest called the cottony cushion scale insect (*Icerya purchasi*) was brought into this country accidentally from Australia. This insect found its way to the citrus groves of California, where it killed many of the trees, causing enormous financial damage. Searching its native Australia, scientists discovered a species of ladybug, the Vedalia beetle (*Rodolia cardinalis*), that was a natural enemy of the invading scale insect. The scientists released millions of the Vedalia ladybugs into the

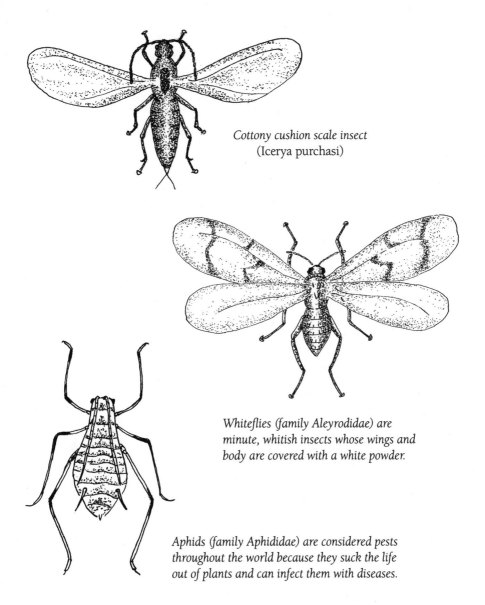

Cottony cushion scale insect
(Icerya purchasi)

Whiteflies (family Aleyrodidae) are minute, whitish insects whose wings and body are covered with a white powder.

Aphids (family Aphididae) are considered pests throughout the world because they suck the life out of plants and can infect them with diseases.

orchards. The ladybugs happily devoured the scale insects and quickly saved an industry that has tremendous value today.

More recently, another import from Australia, the tiny black ladybug (*Delphastus pusillus*), has been pitted against the whitefly, which also threatened citrus orchards, as well as a variety of greenhouse plantings.

The multicolored Asian lady beetle (*Harmonia axyridis*) was also brought into this country for the biological control of aphids. It likes arboreal habitats—trees—and has proven most useful in controlling aphids that infest pecan trees and fruit crops in California, Connecticut, Georgia, Louisiana, and Maryland.

East Coast hemlock trees are presently under attack by sap-sucking insects called adelgids. Once again, ladybugs have come to the rescue. A Japanese ladybug (*Pseudoscymnus tsugae*) is saving these beautiful trees. The industrious insect attacks all stages of the hemlock parasite and thus far has kept pace with the reproductive rate of the adelgids.

This brief history identifies the special relationship that exists between humans and ladybugs. Perhaps no other insect enjoys the protection, and even affection, we extend to them. However, there is something beyond the ladybug's usefulness, a less tangible quality, that brings out our protective instincts toward these pretty little insects. Even children, unaware of the benefits ladybugs provide for crops, are fascinated by them. When they find a ladybug, they coo with delight at the sight of the tiny reddish orange creature with black dots.

Our fascination with ladybugs reached new heights during the mid-twentieth century. By 1973, twenty-nine states, including Delaware, Massachusetts, and Tennessee, had declared the ladybug the state insect. In 1989, after much ado, New York declared the nine-spotted ladybug (*Coccinella novemnotata*) the official state insect. This ladybug has four black spots on each orange wing cover, and one black spot (the ninth) near its neck. None of the approximately seventy kinds of ladybugs found in New York today has these markings. If you look tirelessly for the nine-spotted ladybug, you will not find any. Although it has not been seen in New York since 1970, it nevertheless retains its honored position.

Ladybugs respond to the rhythm of the seasons. As summer fades into autumn, the weather cools. This drop in temperature affects ladybug behavior. Their metabolism slows down as their body temperature falls. In preparation for the cold season, some kinds of ladybugs huddle together in large numbers beneath loose tree bark, in toolsheds, under the shingles of our homes, and in other snug places that will protect them from the harshness of winter. This behavior is sometimes useful to farmers. In the Sierra Nevada, ladybugs that have migrated there and formed huge aggregations at the bases of trees are collected by commercial harvesters, who sell them to farmers by the gallon.

As the air warms in late winter or early spring, ladybugs wake from their dormancy and emerge from their winter shelters. At this time, we often discover them sharing our homes with us. A friend tells me that large swarms of ladybugs find a cool second-floor storage room in her home well suited to their needs as winter wanes.

With the coming of spring, the primary job of ladybugs is to find mates. Their poor eyesight does not hinder this search, because their antennae are designed to detect food, each other, and nonrelated insects. After mating in the spring, the females lay eggs intermittently while continuing their search for pesky insects.

Mating for ladybugs is a periodic event. It's not something they do just once at the beginning of their active season. Often the female mates and feeds simultaneously. The male can't do this because he is perched on the female's back while mating, and the food is out of his reach. The sperm is stored in a special organ in the female's body called the spermatheca, and she can lay a number of egg batches from a single mating. A female may also mate with more than one male before laying a batch of eggs.

Insect development from egg to adult has some fascinating steps. Some insects, such as crickets, develop in a three-stage process (egg, hatchling, and adult) called incomplete, or simple, metamorphosis. The tiny hatchlings look like miniature adults, and the changes that occur during growth and development are not so dramatic. As these insects mature, they change in size, but not much in overall appearance.

Other insects, such as butterflies and moths, develop through a four-stage process called complete metamorphosis. In each of the stages (egg, larva or caterpillar, pupa, and adult), the insect assumes a completely different appearance than it had previously. Ladybug development follows this design of complete metamorphosis.

Ladybugs lay several hundred oval, yellow-orange eggs on the leaves and stems of plants that have large populations of aphids, thrips, mites, mealybugs, and scale insects. These and other soft-bodied insects are food sources for the ladybug larvae that will hatch in several days. A gluelike substance holds the eggs in place. If you are lucky to find small collections of ladybug eggs scattered over the stems and leaves of your houseplants, watch them for a few days, and you will see them darken before hatching.

An emerging rough-skinned hatchling looks like a tiny alligator, rather than the lovely ladybug it is destined to become. Its long, black, segmented body, which is from one-sixteenth to one-eighth inch long, is dotted with red, orange, or yellow spots. Each abdominal segment bears six wartlike clumps adorned with bristly hairs, which probably serve to protect the tiny emergent larva. Along with the bristles, the taste of the larva is so unpleasant that many predators, such as ants, prefer to get their meals elsewhere.

All insect larvae have voracious appetites. Their sole function in life is to eat. Some nutrients are converted into protein, which the larvae use for their

Life cycle of a cricket

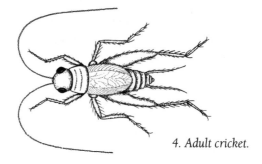

4. Adult cricket.

1. Female lays eggs in soft soil before onset of winter.

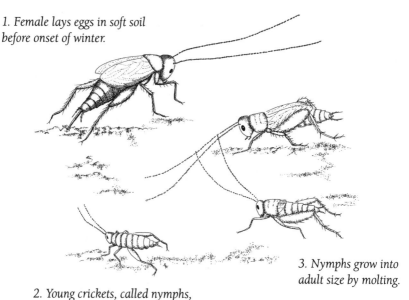

3. Nymphs grow into adult size by molting.

2. Young crickets, called nymphs, hatch in spring.

immediate needs. Other nutrients are stored as fat for later use when the insects are in the pupal stage. Ladybug larvae have strong jaws, which they use to grip aphids while they suck nutrient-laden juices from their bodies. Scientists have determined that the larvae of some ladybug species eat up to five hundred aphids a day, many more than they eat as adults.

During this phase of their development, ladybug larvae grow and develop through a series of three or four molts, developmental stages called instars. As a larva grows larger, its outer skin becomes tight and eventually tears along the back. The larva then crawls free and continues to eat and grow. After the final molt, the larva is about one-half inch long. This is a time full of danger for the developing ladybug, and not all survive. Its predators include lacewing larvae, which are always searching for a meal.

While in the final instar, the larva seeks out a place where it can attach itself to a plant stem or leaf by means of glue and a suckerlike disk at the tip of its abdomen. After a few hours, the old skin splits, revealing the pupa within. The newly exposed pupa darkens as it dries and hardens. It rests on plants where there is abundant food for the emergent adult ladybug.

The pupal phase in the life cycle of the ladybug only appears to be a period of rest, but in fact, it is a time of incredible change. If we could look inside the pupal case, what we would see would bear no resemblance to the wormlike creature it once was. Responding to chemical signals, larval structures break down into a cellular stew. The pupal shell splits, and out of the melange of fat, protein, and other rudimentary materials, a helpless adult ladybug emerges, pushing itself free of the pupal shell with its legs. The length of time spent in the pupal stage varies among ladybug species, but generally it is five to seven days.

Life cycle of the seven-spotted ladybug
(Coccinella septempunctata)

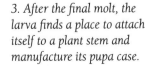

4. Days later, an adult ladybug climbs out of the pupa case.

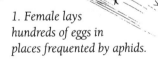

1. Female lays hundreds of eggs in places frequented by aphids.

3. After the final molt, the larva finds a place to attach itself to a plant stem and manufacture its pupa case.

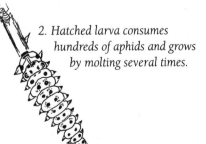

2. Hatched larva consumes hundreds of aphids and grows by molting several times.

The newly emergent ladybug cannot fly. It will take a few hours for its soft wings to dry. The ladybug is at first yellow but slowly changes to its final hue. Spots characteristic of the adult gradually appear. The wing covers harden and expand to protect the delicate wings when the ladybug is resting.

The fully developed adult ladybug may not resemble those pictured in children's storybooks. It will not necessarily have red wing covers with a few well-placed black dots. Depending on the species, ladybugs can be yellow, orange, black, brown, or gray. Some have black dots on their wing covers; others have black splotches or stripes or many black speckles; still others have no markings at all.

Ladybugs have few predators or natural enemies. However, insecticides used to kill the insect pests of house and garden will also kill these delightful allies. The ladybugs' bright colors serve to warn hungry birds and mammals of the unpleasant effects of eating them. When threatened, ladybugs secrete a bitter-tasting fluid from their joints. If would-be predators don't get the "hands-off" message from the ladybug's color, they will not forget the bitter taste, thus saving other ladybugs from being eaten. For humans, the bright colors of the ladybug are not a warning. Instead, we find them attractive. When we see the bright little bugs, we reach out to let them rest on our hands before they fly off to do us good deeds.

THE WORLD OF LADYBUGS

What you will need	Science skills
basic kit	observing
small jar with lid	comparing
graph paper	inferring

Note: If you want to have your own supply of living ladybugs, all you need are some house or patio plants that will attract aphids, a favorite ladybug food. Some good aphid-attracting plants include hibiscus, pansy, rose, and sweet pea. These plants are well suited to growing outside in patio containers or inside the house.

OBSERVATIONS

Capturing a Ladybug. You will need a jar with a lid or a piece of plastic wrap or aluminum foil that you can secure over the mouth with a rubber band. Whichever cap you intend to use, poke a few holes in it for ventilation.

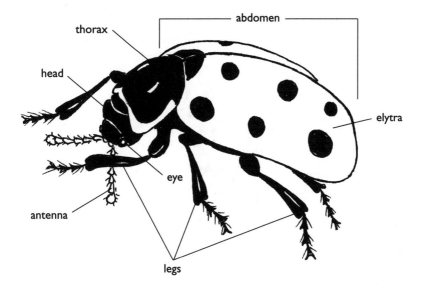

Anatomy of a ladybug

Ladybugs can be found in a variety of places. In the early spring, you may even find them inside the house, perhaps walking along a windowsill. To capture one, put a three-by-five-inch file card in its path. Without hesitation, the ladybug will climb onto it and continue its walk. From here it is easy to coax the ladybug into the jar. If you find a ladybug on a plant, put the mouth of the jar under the leaf or twig it's on, gently tap the supporting foliage, and it will tumble into the jar.

Ladybug Anatomy. With the help of a hand lens, and referring to the illustrations, you can discover a great deal about ladybugs. What color is your ladybug? Does it have spots, blotches, or stripes? If so, how many? How are the markings arranged? Are the colors in the wings or in the wing covers, or are both similarly colored?

Examining the ladybug carefully, how many body parts do you see? Can you identify the head, thorax, and abdomen? The head and thorax together are about one-fourth of the total length of the ladybug. The rest of the ladybug body is made up of the shiny wing covers, called elytra, as well as the abdomen, antennae, and legs. How many antennae are there? Are they as long as the legs? As long as the thorax is wide?

How many legs are there? How does the ladybug use its legs when walking? Are the legs on one side moved forward first, followed by the legs on the other side, or does it move its legs alternately?

Ready to take off, the ladybug opens its red elytra and moves its wings quickly up and down.

How does your ladybug hold its wings when it's not flying? When ladybugs are resting, their wings are folded up and covered by the elytra most of the time. Sometimes you will see the tips of the wings sticking out from under the wing covers. When you release it, watch it when it takes flight. Can you see what it does with the wing covers while it's in flight?

Draw a picture of your ladybug, and make notes that will later help you distinguish it from other ladybugs and possibly identify its species. Note the features it has in common with all ladybugs.

Size. Ladybugs are very small and are difficult to measure with a standard ruler or tape measure. To describe its size, you can compare it to a familiar object, such as a dried split pea, a lentil, or the head of a pin. Using such an object, how big is your ladybug? How many ladybugs could you fit on the bottom of a glass? Perhaps you can trace around it with a pencil so that you have a record of its size for comparison.

Cleanliness. Ladybugs spend a good deal of time using their mouthparts and legs to clean themselves. Watch the process. Is there a pattern to it? Describe it in your notebook. (See Chapter Note 1.)

Larvae. Look carefully on the leaves of plants such as roses, fennel, basil, legumes, or lettuce to find the wormlike ladybug larvae (see the illustration on page 131). Capture a ladybug larva and put it in a jar with plant material and some aphids. Use a hand lens to observe it. What does the larva look like? Describe its shape, its skin, and its color or colors. What distinguishes this larva from other larvae?

Watch it eat. With piercing mouthparts, larvae inject saliva into their prey and suck out the contents. Older larvae can chew whole aphids. How does it use its legs to help? As it grows, it destroys many times its own weight in soft-bodied insects such as aphids, scale insects, and mealybugs. Can you determine what it was eating when you captured it?

If you're lucky, you may see the captured larva go into the pupal phase of its development. Record your observations in your field notebook. Write down any questions you might have about what you observe.

Ladybug Identification. There are a great number of ladybug species, so there is a good chance that you will capture different kinds of ladybugs. This makes your drawings very important. Ladybugs are categorized by their body shape, leg length, color of the wing covers, and type, position, and number of markings. Use the following descriptions to help you determine which kinds of ladybugs you have (see Chapter Note 2).

Two-spotted lady beetle (*Adalia bipunctata*). Just as its name says, this oval ladybug usually has two black spots on its shiny reddish orange wing covers. It is an important predator of aphids, generally in trees and bushes. It frequently enters our homes in the fall, but not in large numbers like *Harmonia axyridis*.

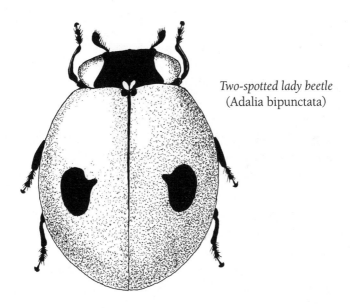

Two-spotted lady beetle
(Adalia bipunctata)

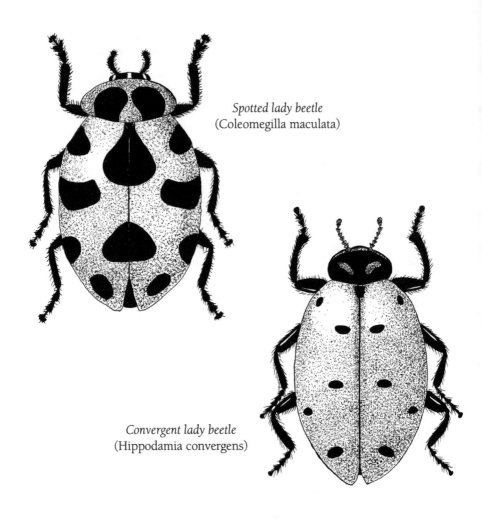

Spotted lady beetle
(Coleomegilla maculata)

Convergent lady beetle
(Hippodamia convergens)

Spotted lady beetle (*Coleomegilla maculata*). This ladybug is slender with long legs and big black markings on its pink or red wing covers. It grows to three-tenths of an inch and is found throughout much of North America.

Convergent lady beetle (*Hippodamia convergens*). This slender, spotted ladybug is one of the most common and abundant species and is considered the "generic ladybug." It gets its name from the two white "hash marks" on its thorax. Although its larvae consume aphids, the number they eat depends on the instar and type of aphid. In the Nevada mountains and the coastal ranges of California, adults gather in great swarms and fly to warm canyons, where they spend the winter. In the higher elevations of the Sierra Nevada, they gather under the snow, where they spend up to nine months. In late February, they return to the valleys.

Vedalia lady beetle (*Rodolia cardinalis*). This ladybug is found mostly in California and Florida but is included here because of its great economic value in the battle against the cottony cushion scale insect. It is red with variable black markings. Unlike the species above, it is covered with very fine, silky hair.

Ashy gray lady beetle (*Olla v-nigrum*). The species name has been changed from *abdominalis* to *v-nigrum*. You can find this ladybug in most areas of the United States. It is nearly circular in shape. Some are pale yellow with many black spots, but others may be gray or beige. Another color form is black with two red spots. Walnut aphids are a favorite food, but it will also eat other aphids, jumping plant lice (called psyllids), and whiteflies.

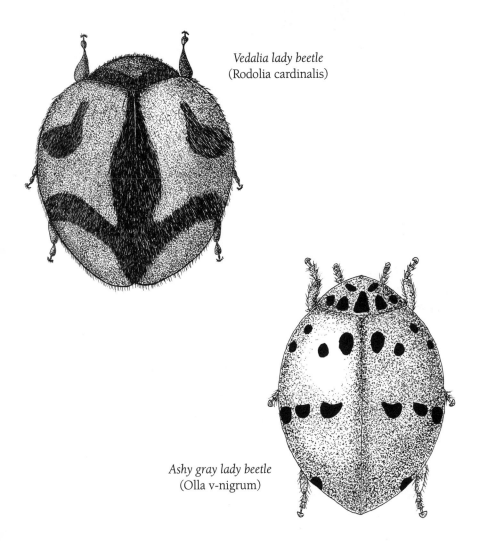

Vedalia lady beetle
(Rodolia cardinalis)

Ashy gray lady beetle
(Olla v-nigrum)

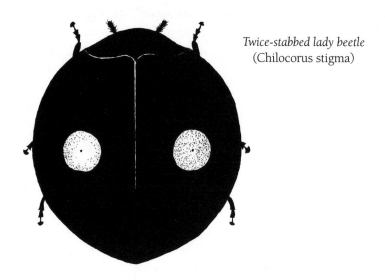

Twice-stabbed lady beetle
(Chilocorus stigma)

Twice-stabbed lady beetle (*Chilocorus stigma*). This round, shiny black ladybug has two bright red spots on its wing covers. Its name comes from the red spots, one on each wing cover. It is found throughout the United States.

Yellow-spotted lady beetle (*Hyperaspis signata*). These tiny, oval ladybugs are predominantly black with markings that range from orange to deep red. Sometimes they are marked with stripes. You will find them on the East Coast, from New York to Florida, and west to Texas.

Multicolored Asian lady beetle (*Harmonia axyridis*) and Seven-spotted lady beetle (*Coccinella septempunctata*). These two introduced species are now among the most common species found in the United States.

Ladybug Diet. Some ladybugs specialize in the types of prey they eat; others are more general. Several members of the order Homoptera, such as aphids, whiteflies, scale insects, and mealybugs, are common foods for ladybugs. Mites, thrips, newly hatched caterpillars, and an assortment of beetle larvae add variety as well as protein to their diet.

Aphids. In your observations of ladybugs, you likely will find one of the most infamous plant pests—aphids, also known as plant lice. Aphids are among the choice foods for ladybugs. Look for them on the leaves, stems, and flowers of various plants. When you find a colony, examine them with a hand lens. Make a drawing. Describe the aphids' eyes, antennae, and legs. Do the aphids have wings, or are they wingless? How do they move through the colony? Do you see tubes on the back? (See Chapter Note 3.) What color are the aphids? Although aphids come in other colors, such as red, most of them are green, which provides the camouflage they need to avoid predators. Are they as big as a pinhead or two pinheads?

Aphids use hollow, needlelike mouthparts to pierce plant leaves and stems, then suck out the sugary sap. Can you see this needlelike projection? From the sap, aphids produce a thick, sweet substance called honeydew, which they excrete. Honeydew combined with body protein makes aphids a hearty meal for ladybugs, which have been known to eat as many as a hundred aphids in a day.

Are the aphids feeding? Are their feeding tubes or beaks stuck into the plant stem or leaf? Touch an aphid and make it move. What does it do with its feeding tube as it moves? How does it move its antennae as it travels on the plant?

EXPLORATIONS

Survival Techniques. Carefully remove a ladybug from a plant and put it on its back on a flat surface. If you disturb a ladybug, it often will fold up its legs and drop as if dead, playing possum in a most deceptive manner. It will remain in this attitude of rigid death from a few seconds to a minute or two, then begin to claw the air with its six legs in an effort to turn right side up. How long does your ladybug remain in this apparently lifeless position? What do you think is the advantage of this behavior? How does it get itself right side up? How long does it take? Try this with a few other ladybugs. What is the average time it takes for a ladybug to right itself?

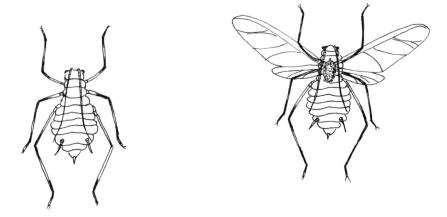

Aphids may or may not have wings, but all have piercing mouthparts that are tucked under the body when not in use.

Touch the ladybug's antennae. How do they respond? Write descriptions of what you have observed in your notebook.

Another defense mechanism is chemical. Do you see droplets of yellow or orange fluid? Ladybugs give out a horrible-tasting fluid from the joints in their legs that keeps enemies from eating them.

Pattern of Movement. Put the ladybug on a large piece of paper. As it moves on the paper, follow it with a felt-tipped pen, drawing the path it makes. Try this with other ladybugs. Use a different-colored marker for each ladybug. Do the paths resemble each other? Do they follow a straight line, or do they make many little turns as they go along?

Climbing Behavior. Hold a twig in its natural position. Put ladybugs in various places on the twig. What do they do? Try this several times and record what happens. You may want to support the twig by sticking it into a ball of Play-Doh.

Looking for a Meal. How ladybugs find aphids on plants is a question that many entomologists have pondered. Their observations have led to some interesting conclusions. Aphids generally dine near the veins of leaves, on the new growth at the tip of a plant, or inside little nooks and crevices, such as at the joints of plant stems. Ladybugs instinctively know they should spend more time investigating these parts of the plant in their search for aphids. Look at a plant on which you have discovered aphids. Do you see them in any special place on the leaves? Since ladybugs feed on aphids, what would be the most productive strategies for the ladybugs?

Take a leaf that is infested with aphids, hold it above a large piece of paper, and gently blow on it (don't puff; do it the way you would blow on a window-pane or a pair of glasses to steam them up). Some aphids should tumble off the leaf and end up scattered on the paper. Place two or three ladybugs in the center of the paper. What kind of search pattern (walking path) do the ladybugs follow? How long does it take them to find the aphids? Watch what happens after a ladybug eats an aphid. Usually the ladybug will turn about and carefully search the area near where it found the first aphid. This is a useful behavior, because aphids usually occur in clusters in nature, and this enables the ladybug to easily find more.

Attracting Ladybugs to Your Garden. If you would like to attract ladybugs to your garden, dill, fennel, dandelion, wild carrot, and yarrow are some good plants to cultivate. The presence of ladybugs will reduce the need to use chemicals to control aphid populations.

Raising Ladybugs in Your House. Find a plant with aphids on it. Make a cage for the plant out of fine wire mesh. Add ladybugs to the plant. Put the cage in a bright location, but not in direct sunlight. In time, the ladybugs will mate and lay eggs.

You can observe the development of the ladybugs from eggs to larvae to adults. Keep a record of this development in your notebook, drawing the changes that occur.

The newly developed ladybugs will need food. You can supply the hungry beetles with aphids by cutting infested stems from other plants and placing the stems in the cage with the developing ladybugs.

Effects of Ladybugs on Aphid Population. Find a plant that has several aphids living on it. Count the number of aphids, then loosely wrap the plant with plastic wrap. Is there a daily increase in the number of aphids on a plant? Count the aphids every day for three weeks. Make a graph like the one below to chart your findings. How many aphids would you have in three months; six months; a year?

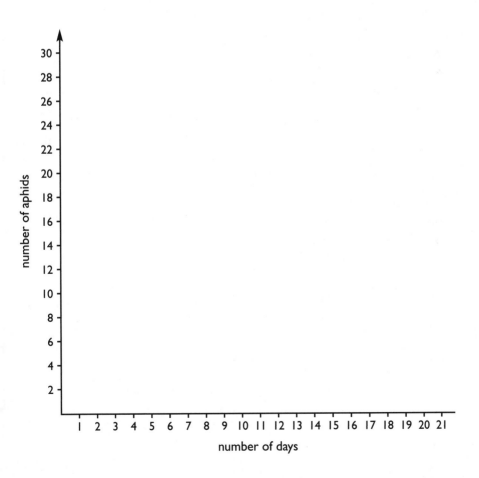

Now add two ladybugs to the plant. Continue to count the number of aphids every day for three more weeks. Chart your findings on a second graph. Compare the two graphs. What generalizations can you make about the relationship between ladybugs and aphids?

CHAPTER NOTES

I. The ladybug bathes itself by cleaning its front legs and antennae with its mandibles, removing grains of dust and pollen. It cleans its middle and hind legs by rubbing the two on the same side back and forth against each other. It cleans its wings by brushing them between the edges of the wing covers and the lower portion of its hind legs.

2. Most of the ladybug groups described here are found throughout the United States. There are many other groups that live primarily in California, New Mexico, Arizona, and Florida.

3. The tubes located on the back of the aphid secrete a waxy substance that gums up the mouthparts of a would-be attacker.

CHAPTER 8

Wasps

ARCHITECTS IN THE ATTIC

On a warm October day, you may walk into your garage or toolshed and find a slender-waisted, gold-banded wasp basking in a shaft of warm autumn sunlight. On such a day, you may also hear the soft humming of wasps in the rafters overhead. You can also expect to find a few wasps buzzing under the porch or in the attic. You may find some strange, tubular structures made of dried mud fastened to walls or under the eaves. They exist singly or in groups that resemble organ pipes. Occasionally you might see a large paper nest the size of a basketball dangling from a tree. In warm weather, these nests are usually attended by buzzing wasps, which discourage any interference by executing a few close, swooping dives around an intruder's ears. Sometimes these insects are called hornets, although this name properly applies to only one group of wasps.

Wasps are not considered as interesting—or as safe a research subject—as many other insects, such as butterflies, dragonflies, or fireflies, and thus they are not studied as extensively. What is generally known about wasps is that they sting, they build a variety of odd-looking shelters, and they invade our summer picnics. But what exactly is a wasp? Which of the many winged, buzzing insects that we see are wasps? Do all wasps sting? How long do they live? Are wasps even the slightest bit beneficial to humans?

Wasps are insects, which tells us their bodies are divided into three sections: head, chest or thorax, and abdomen. They have two pairs of transparent wings, with the hind pair smaller than the front pair. This places them in the order Hymenoptera. Other members of the order, bees and ants,

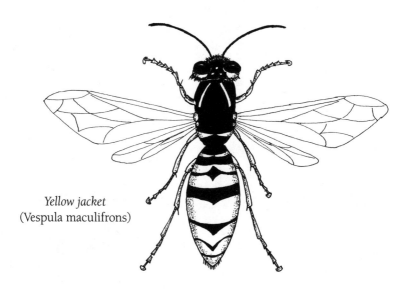

Yellow jacket
(Vespula maculifrons)

You can recognize ants even with wings, because their antennae are strongly elbowed.

may resemble wasps in physical and/or behavioral characteristics, but wasps are distinguished from their cousins in that bees are covered by branched, feathery hair, whereas the hairs of wasps are simple and unbranched, and all ants have distinctly elbowed antennae.

There are about eighteen thousand species of wasps, making wasp identification difficult, even for an expert. New species are still being identified, and there also are similarities among non-wasps, such as some flies that mimic wasp color as part of their defense strategies (see Chapter Note 1).

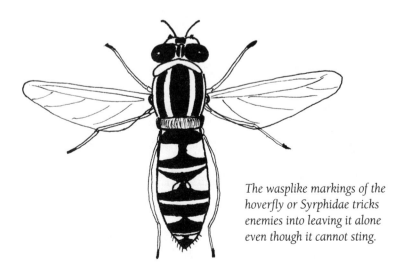

The wasplike markings of the hoverfly or Syrphidae tricks enemies into leaving it alone even though it cannot sting.

Entomologists, scientists who study insects, have divided wasps into two groups: those that fold their wings like a fan, and those that lay the wings down the middle of the back without pleating them. This latter habit is also found in most bees and winged ants.

Wasps also can be divided into two main groups according to their lifestyle: social wasps and solitary wasps. Those that live in communities are labeled social wasps and belong to the family Vespidae. This group includes the familiar yellow jackets, hornets, and paper wasps (*Polistes* sp.). The vespid wasps live in well-organized colonies. Some live in small groups, but the majority gather in large congregations with thousands of individuals.

Yellow jackets and hornets (*Vespula* sp.) both are aggressive wasps. Hornets, especially the bald-faced hornets *(Vespula maculata),* are found throughout North America. Their smoky black wings and white-and-black head pattern make them relatively easy to distinguish. They are well known for their large, globular paper nests, built from a mixture of wood pulp and saliva, with the doorway at the bottom. These nests can be found hanging from trees or attached to buildings. Their saliva contains a gluelike substance that causes the wood fibers in the pulp to adhere to one another while being chewed. With modifications of these techniques, humans were able to build a very successful paper industry.

Yellow jackets and hornets begin their communal life in the spring, when a mated female is awakened by the warming weather. She has survived the winter by hibernating in a sheltered place under some leaf litter, in a woodpile, or on a stone wall. Her first job is to find a suitable nest site and begin its construction. From spring until autumn, she lays eggs that produce the workers that help repair and modify the nest as needed and tend the young. As time progresses through the summer, older workers become housekeepers and are fed by other specialized workers called foragers. It is not possible for the casual observer to distinguish foragers from workers, since they resemble each other. The foragers feed on plant nectar and fruits. Plant juices are stored in sacs in the digestive tract called crops and are carried back to the nest, where the forager wasps regurgitate the nutrients and pass them on to the workers, which in turn feed the larvae. Wasp larvae that are being fed or stimulated release drops of liquid relished by the workers. Sometimes the workers will stimulate the larvae and drink the liquid, but not offer food. This behavior results in the death of developing wasps. Workers that do this are referred to as social parasites.

When temperatures cool at night, the queen's eggs produce males called drones. As winter approaches, young queens and drones leave their nests and

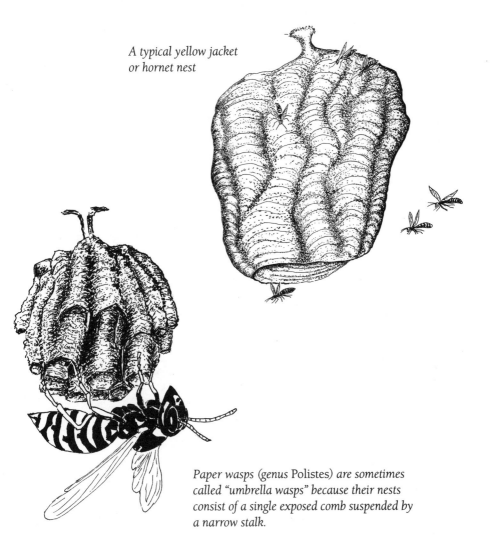

A typical yellow jacket or hornet nest

Paper wasps (genus Polistes*) are sometimes called "umbrella wasps" because their nests consist of a single exposed comb suspended by a narrow stalk.*

perform a mating dance high in the sky. After mating, the queens kill their mates and seek shelter for the winter. Only the queen survives the winter. All the workers, foragers, and drones die off before the onset of the cold season. In the spring, the nest-building and egg-laying cycle begins anew.

Other wasp architects that make their nests close to us are the paper wasps (*Polistes* sp.). These are also social wasps (family Vespidae), but they build a different kind of nest, consisting of paper combs placed beneath the eaves of houses and in sheltered areas such as garages, sheds, and other out-buildings. These open-celled combs, when completed, resemble upside-down goblets or wine glasses secured by their stems.

Paper wasps build colonial nests, but they have a much less structured organization than the yellow jackets and hornets. The social organization of paper wasps consists of a group of cooperating females. Some believe these wasps are more tolerant of humans and will not bother us unless they see us as a threat to their community. The *Polistes* probably don't fly around sweaty humans or their picnic tables in search of moisture or sugar the way *Vespula* species do, but *Polistes canadensis*, a large wasp with a reddish brown body and brown wings, shows strong defensive aggression among females of its species and is also aggressive toward humans.

Other types of wasps live alone rather than in communities. The black and yellow mud dauber (*Sceliphron caementarium*) and blue-black mud dauber (*Chalybion californicum*) are members of this reclusive group. They belong to the family Sphecidae, which includes the vast majority of wasp species.

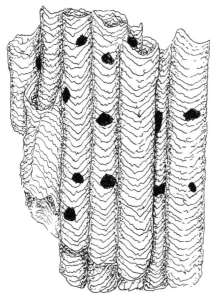

Abandoned mud dauber (family Sphecidae) nests are commonly found under the eaves of houses and other sheltered locations.

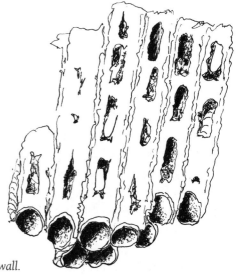

Flat side of an abandoned mud dauber nest after removal from a wall.

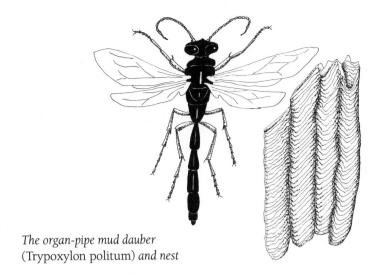

The organ-pipe mud dauber
(Trypoxylon politum) *and nest*

The organ-pipe mud dauber (*Trypoxylon politum*) can be found throughout the United States. Like many other solitary wasps, its behavior is focused on offspring that it will never see. The lifestyle of these wasps is simple when compared to that of the social wasps: there are no queens, only males and females.

Early in the autumn, after mating, the female mud daubers busily search for a suitable place to build a nest. They look for such sites in garages, toolsheds, attics, and other places where the nest will be protected, especially from wet weather. Once such a site is found, construction of the nest begins.

To gather the required material, the winged masons frequent the edges of puddles, where they gather mouthfuls of mud, or dry dirt when mud cannot be found. The wasp mixes these materials with saliva until she has produced a substance that acts like cement. Often a completed nest shows a range of color from light gray to black, depending on what substances are dissolved in the mud. The differences in color also can indicate that the mud was taken from a variety of sources. After many trips to sources of mortar, a foundation for the nest is completed.

Now the wasp begins the construction of a vertical tube. With her jaws, she forms mud balls, which she lays at the nest site. She then spreads each ball, using her mandibles like a mason's trowel, into the tubular cell that will be the nest for her developing offspring. Although the cells vary in length, they average about an inch long and one-eighth inch thick. Sometimes a wasp will build her nest at a site used seasons before by another wasp. This creates a cluster of tubes, known as organ pipes.

Upon completion of a tube, the mud dauber leaves the nest site in search of spiders (other species of solitary wasps search for different types of prey). Once she finds a spider, the mud dauber stings it until it is paralyzed but not killed. The spiders are rendered immobile so that they cannot struggle with the hungry wasp larvae or escape from the cell. After each spider is paralyzed, the mud dauber carries it back to the nest, where she stuffs it into the open tube. She repeats this process until the tube is filled with spiders. This arrangement provides fresh food for the larvae or grubs as soon as they emerge. Stocking the nest in this way is sometimes called mass provisioning and gives these wasps the nickname of hunting wasps.

Exactly when, in the process of stuffing the cell with spiders, the wasp lays her egg is not known for sure. Some observers have recorded that the wasp laid an egg on the first spider brought into the cell, others that the egg was laid on the second or third spider, and still others that the egg was placed on the last spider brought into the nest tube. Once the cell is full of potential food for the wasp offspring and the egg has been laid, the cell is sealed. Most solitary wasps, after thus stocking their nests, laying their eggs, and sealing the cells, never return and will not live to see their young.

At the end of a workday, if the cell was not completely filled, the wasp fashions a thin cover to temporarily close it. Following her rest period, she removes the seal and continues her work. Additional tubes are constructed in a similar fashion, each receiving an egg and similar provisions. All of this activity is carried out by a lone female solitary wasp that has never seen the work performed by another wasp.

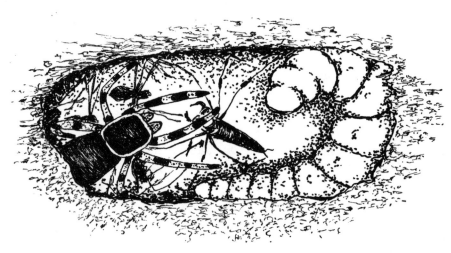

Mud daubers actually pack an empty cell full of food for their young.

THE ANIMALS

When the young hatch, they are grublike and bear no resemblance to the adult wasps they will become. At this stage in their development, the wasps look like white maggots. They lack compound eyes, wings, and legs, but even at this early stage, their bodies are segmented. The larvae eat by piercing the spiders and sucking them dry. Later in their development, the larvae eat the remaining parts of the spiders.

By this time, their jaws, or mandibles, will have developed adequately for the job. It takes about three weeks for a wasp larva to consume all the spiders in its cell. It will remain in the cell for about eight months (October to May), a long larval period.

In April or May, due to the warming temperatures of spring, rapid changes begin to occur, and the larva enters the next phase of its development, becoming a pupa. Secure in a silken cocoon, which is firmly attached to the cell wall, the pupa develops into an adult. Unlike the larval stage of development, in which there is voracious feeding, the pupal stage appears to be one of silent rest. In actuality, it is a period of incredible change. If you were to look inside the cocoon, what you would see would bear no resemblance to the architect that built it. Responding to chemical signals, larval structures break down into a cellular stew. Out of this melange of fat, protein, and rudimentary materials, a helpless wasp with crumpled wings takes the place of the larva that built the cocoon. The process of developing from pupa to adult takes about four days. When the developmental changes are complete, the adult wasp frees itself from its silken wrap but remains in the cell for about a week. It then gnaws its way through the mud plug at the entrance of the cell. Upon emerging, the wasp is a fully developed mason with a license to build. It cuts its way through the door and freely explores its surroundings.

The wasp's first flight may take it far from the nest and it may never return. However, some mud daubers will come back for shelter, since the nests are located in protected places. If you have a returning mud dauber, you may want to encourage its presence by leaving some honey in a small dish. This will allow you to spend some time observing its behavior.

The newly emerged solitary wasp has no bonds with the wasps that developed in adjacent cells. Also, it will never know the wasp that built its nest and provisioned it with food. Following preliminary explorations, the female wasps begin looking for suitable nest sites and the cycle repeats itself, as it has done for millions of years.

At the end of each season, as each nest is abandoned, several varieties of smaller wasps often move into these nests. These newcomers soften the walls with their saliva, then break them down and throw out the contents. They restock the cells, replaster the nests, and call them home.

There are a few species of solitary wasps that supply their nests with a minimal amount of food, bringing it to the nest for the hatchlings and surviving long enough to feed their young. This strategy, called progressive provisioning, resembles the way birds bring food to their young.

Entomologists know from the evidence left in the fossil record that solitary wasps have been around much longer than communal wasps. They believe that the first step in the evolution of social wasps was the provisioning by adult solitary wasps of the nests in which they laid eggs. The next step in this development seems to be represented by solitary wasps that supply minimal amounts of food to the developing larvae. The adults of this group return to the nest from time to time with more food. In some species, the mother feeds the young herself, while in other species, females other than the mother prepare the food by chewing it into a paste before feeding it to the developing larvae.

Although these developments are seen as the beginning of social behavior in a wasp colony, solitary wasps are not in decline. Entomologists who have spent time in the field tell us there are several thousand species of solitary wasps in the world. Some of these belong to the hunting group, and you are likely to find them in or around your home.

In the larger picture, wasps help control the spider population, and some help control the huge numbers of plant-eating insects that are the scourge of agricultural crops.

THE WORLD OF WASPS

What you will need	Science skills
basic kit	*observing*
	inferring

Caution: Always exercise great care around wasps and their nests, using gloves and tweeers as appropriate. Even dead wasps are capable of stinging you.

OBSERVATIONS

Wasp Species

Vespid wasps (family Vespidae). This family is known informally as the social wasps.

Paper wasps (**Polistes sp.**). These wasps are reddish black or brown, with yellow rings on head and body. They are common throughout the United

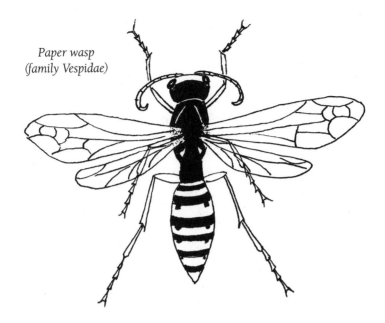

Paper wasp
(family Vespidae)

States. You can find their small-stemmed, open nests on roof overhangs, porch ceilings, and the underside of similar surfaces. The nest is uncovered.

Bald-faced hornet (**Vespula maculata**). This species has a black-and-white pattern on its face. It builds pear-shaped nests suspended from trees and shrubs. Probably the most well-known hornet, it ranges throughout North America. In fact, this immigrant, which arrived here sometime before 1840, is the largest social wasp in North America.

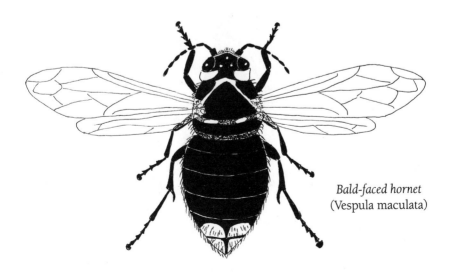

Bald-faced hornet
(Vespula maculata)

Giant hornet (**Vespa crabro germana**). This species has a bright yellow abdomen with dark cross bands and small spots. It is found in the eastern United States, west to the Dakotas. It is the only vespine in the New World that is brown with yellow markings. It builds globular, covered nests under a porch, deck, or roof.

Yellow jacket (**Vespula *sp.***). The abdomens of these wasps are banded black and yellow. They build globular, covered nests in trees and shrubs close to the ground. *Vespula* also nest in the ground. You might not want to wear shorts while cutting the grass.

Sphecid wasps (family Sphecidae). This is a very large family with more than eleven hundred species in North America. It is divided into many subfamilies.

Organ-pipe mud daubers (subfamily Trypoxyloninae). These wasps make tubular nests, although some nest in structural cavities in buildings. All of these wasps stock their nests with spiders.

Thread-waisted wasps (subfamily Sphecinae). This subfamily includes wasps in the tribe Sceliphronini. Most of these wasps are mud daubers that make their nests of mud and supply them with paralyzed spiders for the larvae. They include the black and yellow mud dauber (*Sceliphron caementarium*) and the blue-black mud dauber (*Chalybion californicum*).

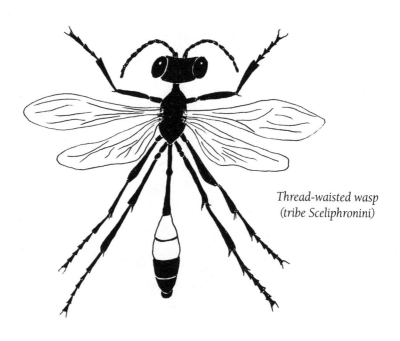

Thread-waisted wasp
(tribe Sceliphronini)

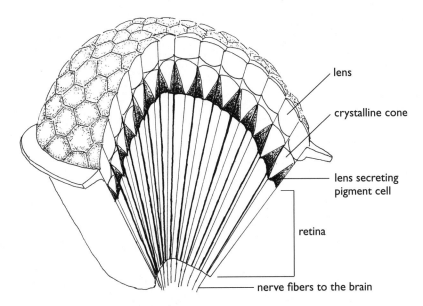

lens

crystalline cone

lens secreting
pigment cell

retina

nerve fibers to the brain

Cutaway view of the compound eye of an insect

A Close Look at a Wasp. If you find a dead wasp, you can examine it with the help of a hand lens.

Eyes. A wasp has one large compound eye on each side of the head. These eyes are made up of thousands of tiny windows called facets. Each facet, like an individual eye, is complete with a lens and has its own nerve pathways to the brain. Our eyes, which are designed for detecting very fine detail, have only one lens each but many nerve receptors behind that lens. Like all insect eyes, the wasp's eyes are designed primarily to detect the motion of small objects. In addition to the compound eyes, the wasp has three simple eyes, called ocelli, on the top of the forehead. These eyes cannot form an image, but they are sensitive to light. Scientists have discovered that wasps are guided by color, so if you plan to be in an area frequented by wasps, it is better to wear khaki or other dull-toned clothes.

Wings. Generally, the first indication that a wasp is in the area is the sound of its whirring wings. Although a few wasp species are wingless, most have two pairs of membranous wings. The smaller hind wings have a row of small hooks along their leading edge, which attach to a fold on the trailing edge of the front wings. Each wing is divided into compartments of different sizes and shapes. Entomologists use these compartments, or cells, along with other traits to determine the species of a particular wasp. Wasp wings can

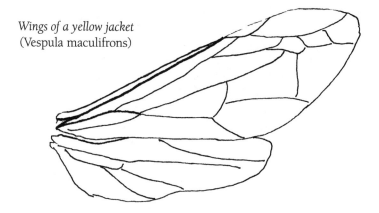

Wings of a yellow jacket
(Vespula maculifrons)

propel a wasp through the air at thirty miles per hour as they beat about 110 times a second.

Sting. The sting is a modified egg-laying organ of the female wasp. As a weapon, this organ, called the ovipositor, injects products of the poison glands into the skin of a victim. Each species has its own formula for the toxin it can inject. The species that are incapable of stinging humans vastly outnumber those that can. Wasps of most species will attempt to sting if held—even males go through the motions—but most are unable to penetrate the skin. Female Hymenoptera are capable of inflicting a sting, but not all can sting humans. Some parasitic wasps (family Ichneumonidae) can deliver a wallop, although there is little chance for them to sting people that aren't collecting them. The

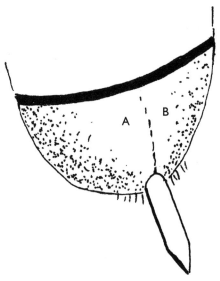

The wasp sting is housed in the abdomen. The two halves of the abdomen casing open slightly to allow the stinging apparatus to emerge.

Paper wasp antenna
(Vespula)

Harvester ant antenna
(Pheidole)

solitary wasps use their sting to paralyze prey. They seldom bother us unless they are provoked or when paralyzing food for their larvae. The social wasps, the hornets and yellow jackets, are more aggressive, using their sting as a defense, and they will sting without much provocation. It is these wasps that can cause a disturbance at backyard picnics.

Antennae. These appendages are very important. Unlike many other insects, which have taste organs on the mouthparts or, like butterflies, moths, and flies, have taste organs on the tarsi (portion of leg segment), wasps have their taste organs on their antennae. They provide the wasp with information about its environment through the senses of touch, smell, and perhaps hearing. The wasp antenna has a ball and socket similar to what you will find on a boom-box antenna, which helps the wasp rotate it in all directions. Although antennae differ among wasp species, all have a stiff portion close to the head and a flexible tip where the sense organs are located.

Mud Dauber Nests. Most mud daubers make tubular nests, although the nests of *Sceliphron caementarium* are not tubular, but rectangular. Look for mud dauber nests on the walls of garages, sheds, and barns, especially around windows and doorways. Roof overhangs, rafters, attics, and other places sheltered from stormy weather also make desirable nest sites. A particularly favored spot will have a nest or nests from previous years. The condition of these nests will vary with exposure and age. You may discover a single pipe or a cluster of pipes. A cluster does not indicate the presence of social wasps, but that solitary wasp architects found a particularly favorable location. Mud daubers may build several nests in one season. The nests may be in different locations, or the female mason may add tubes to existing nests.

Where is the nest located? On the north, south, west, or east side of the building? What is the advantage of this location? Is there only one pipe, or are several glued together? What color are they? Is the color uniform throughout? Is there a pattern on the pipes? Are they smooth or rough? How big are they?

Measure the length and width of each pipe. If there is more than one pipe, how big is the set?

Are there large holes made by emerging wasps? Tubes completed during the most recent nesting season will not have holes in them, because they still hold undeveloped wasps. A small hole in the tube is an indication of probable parasite invasion.

Record your findings in your notebook. Make a drawing or take a photograph of the nest and surrounding area.

Observing Mud Daubers. The mud daubers are not aggressive and will not bother you if they do not see you as threatening to them or their nest. The black and yellow mud daubers (*Sceliphron caementarium*) are the most plentiful species. Their beautiful bodies are a rich black with golden yellow stripes. In the late spring, you may have an opportunity to observe these masons at work. It will take some hours of dedicated watching to learn some fascinating aspects about the lives of these wasps. Watch them walk. How do they hold their wings? Do you see them stretch? Does more than one occupy a place such as a windowsill at one time? Is there more than one wasp in the area of the construction site? Are the others all black and yellow mud daubers?

Frequently the first hint of mud daubers in the area is the soft whir of their wings. You may hear this from late spring to midsummer. If they choose a place around your home to build their nests, you will be able to observe them as they work. You may even see the female carry a ball of mud in her mandibles to the nest site. When she leaves the nest site for the mud source, how long does it take her to return? Where is this source located? How large are the mud balls? How does she spread the mud? How long does it take her to spread the mud of one ball?

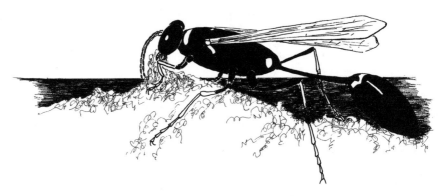

A black and yellow mud dauber (Sceliphron caementarium) *gathers mud at the edge of a pond.*

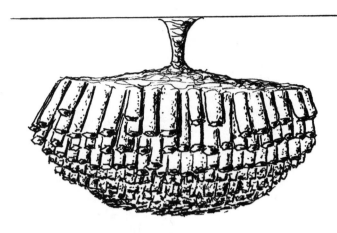

Abandoned paper wasp nest

Paper Wasp Nests. Look for the open, short-stemmed nests of paper wasps (*Polistes* sp.) on a porch ceiling, roof overhang, or other building sites. Write a description of any nests you find. How many cells are there? Are they empty? Do some of the cells contain larvae? Some of the cells may be covered.

Yellow Jacket and Hornet Nests. Although paper wasps are very tolerant of human activity, yellow jackets and hornets are more easily disturbed. Wait until after the first hard frost before handling the nest of any wasp. Prior to this time, they still may shelter live wasps, which are always ready to defend their homes with painful stings.

Polistes build their nests beneath eaves, but the nests of their tropical relatives are found in trees and shrubs. Certain hornets and yellow jackets build their nests in the ground. Wasp nests are made of wood pulp that the wasps manufacture by mixing saliva with bits of wood taken from weathered boards or logs. A major difference between the nests of hornets and yellow jackets is that those of yellow jackets are finer in texture. These nests deteriorate as winter sets in and the weather becomes increasingly harsh.

Once you have found a nest, describe it and its location. What is its shape? What color is it? Is the color uniform throughout the nest? Is the covering of the nest layered, or is it a single sheet of paper? Where is the entrance located? How big is it?

The layers of paper do not lie on top of one another. Air spaces are left between these to provide insulation. This helps the wasps keep the temperature of the nest at about 86 degrees F (30 degrees C). If the inside temperature falls much below this, some of the wasps begin to contract their flight muscles. This raises their metabolic rate, which produces heat. Should the temperature

WASPS **159**

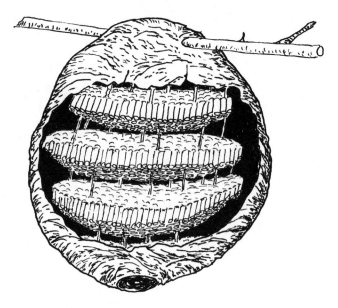

Cutaway view of a bald-faced hornet nest

inside the nest become too high, some wasps spread water droplets among the combs. Fanning their wings induces the cooling effects of evaporation.

You may wonder why the wasps don't add more insulation to the nest. To do so, the wasps would have to spend a great deal of energy to find bits of wood and chew it into a pulp. They would need to spread the resulting paste around the nest to make new layers. These activities would require tremendous energy and valuable time needed for other tasks, such as repairing the existing layers, capturing food for developing larvae, and warding off invaders or nest predators.

EXPLORATIONS

Eating Behavior. The best time to try this exploration is late in the summer. When these Hymenoptera swarm to our picnic tables, they are searching for food at season's end. The things they normally eat, such as caterpillars, flies, and maggots, are dwindling, so they turn to an easier and more abundant source of nutrition.

Put some tiny pieces of uncooked meat in one dish and some small pieces of sweet fruit in another, and place them on a table in your yard. How long does it take for wasps to arrive at the table? Record their behavior. How do they use their antennae? Describe the behavior as they detect each food's flavor through touch.

Now put some sweet fruit juice in a saucer. How does the wasp drink the liquid? Like a puppy? Or does it use a strawlike device like a butterfly? What happens if another wasp comes to the dish? After drinking the liquid, does it clean its feet? How does it do it?

Wasp Interactions. A wasp uses its antennae to determine whether another wasp is a member of its colony. Observe a meeting between two wasps. What do they do with their antennae? Another characteristic activity among wasps is the interchange of materials, such as food and secretions, between individuals.

Collecting Wasp Nests. Unless you want to incur the wrath of the inhabitants, do not try to remove a wasp nest from its support until after the first hard frost. Prior to this time, the nests may shelter live wasps, which are always ready to defend their homes with painful stings. By this time, all except the queens of the social wasp colonies will have been killed by the subfreezing temperatures. The mud dauber females also will have found shelter from the killing weather. These wasps, if lucky, will remain protected until spring arrives. Then the surviving females will begin the cycle of life again.

Examining a Mud Dauber Nest. You can remove the old nest from its support by placing a spatula between the nest and the wall, rafter, or roof. How many cells are in the tube? If you found a group of tubes, are there the same number of cells in each tube? What is the size of the cells? Are they empty? If they are not empty, examine the contents. A hand lens will help. Are there cocoons in the cells? Describe them. How big are they? Are they translucent or opaque? Leathery or delicate? Can you see the remains of spiders or other food left for the developing larvae? Did you find small white pellets? (See Chapter Note 2.)

Examining a Yellow Jacket or Hornet Nest. Cut away one side of the nest so you can have a view of the inside of the nest from top to bottom. Is the color of the covering uniform? What might explain any variations you may notice? Peel off a piece of the covering. How many layers are there?

The number of tiers inside the nest depends on the age and size of the colony. How many tiers are in the nest? Are they of equal size? How are the tiers separated from each other? All of the cells in a tier open downward. How many cells are there in each tier? Are there any signs of the larvae that pupated in the cells? What is the shape of the cocoons?

Each egg is glued to the cell wall to prevent it from falling out. After hatching, the tail end of the larva is kept in the cell, and its head is able to protrude out of the opening so that it can be fed by the workers. Some young larvae tumble out of their cells, and the workers simply carry them out of the

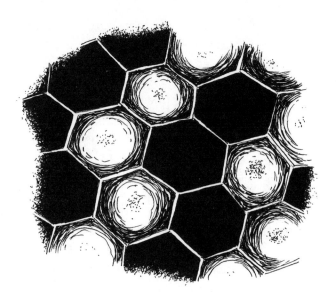

Cells of social wasps' nests

nest. When fully grown, the larvae spin suits of tough, translucent silk that adheres to the cell wall. You may see the remains of these cocoons protruding from several cells in each tier.

The wasp nest may have been used for shelter by other insects, such as flies. You may find evidence of insects that fed on the remaining pupae or simply found shelter in the nest.

CHAPTER NOTES

1. Many adult syrphid flies (Syrphidae) or hoverflies are brightly colored and resemble various wasps. They are often common around flowers and frequently hover a great deal. They prey on aphids and other garden and agricultural pests, and thus are extremely beneficial.

2. In old mud dauber nests, you may see dry, white oval pellets in the cocoons. They are extremely small and may measure from one to one and one-half millimeters. Because there are so many of them, a collection of them is easily seen. These pellets are made of uric acid crystals. During the larval and pupal stages, the mud dauber accumulated insoluble uric acid in the body cavity, and this was removed during the first week of its adult life.

CHAPTER 9

House Mice

LONG TAILS AND POINTED NOSES

Two people see a mouse darting across the floor. One is fascinated by the cute little beast. The other is terrified and makes a great deal of fuss. Two very different reactions to the same creature. Why is this so universally true?

If you were to search for an answer to this question, you would find that it is because most people know very little about mice, even though they have been part of our lives for a very long time. When asked to describe a mouse, people will usually say it is little and furry and has a long, hairless tail. Most recognize it as a rodent, a close relative of the rat, which they despise. For some reason, when people have few reliable facts to go on, they fall prey to fears based on myths and folk tales. This has happened with bats, sharks, spiders, snakes, and mice. Perhaps it is time to get to know our little companions, some of whom have traveled with us all over the earth. They are so close to humans in their biology that they have been studied in laboratories as a human substitute and have helped scientists discover a great deal about diseases that plague us and probe the mysteries of genetic flaws. In one typical year, the National Institutes of Health used eight hundred thousand mice to help scientists explore many of those mysteries. The species used in research is the house mouse (*Mus musculus*), but these are laboratory strains.

There are many different kinds of mice, and they live in a variety of habitats. The golden mouse (*Ochrotomys nuttalli*) lives in moist thickets of the Southeast. The eastern harvest mouse (*Reithrodontomys humulis*) prefers fields and wet meadows. The oldfield mouse (*Peromyscus polionotus*) of Georgia, Alabama, and Florida prefers to stay close to sandy beaches. The plains pocket mouse (*Perognathus flavescens*) gets its common name from the small, fur-lined cheek pouches that open externally on either side of the mouth. It lives in open, sandy areas from North Dakota to northern Texas. Two well-known mice that are part-time commensals with humans are the white-footed mouse (*Peromyscus leucopus*) and the deer mouse (*Peromyscus maniculatus*). A commensal is any organism that lives with or on another and gains shelter, food, or some other essential need without harming or benefiting the host. In the wild, these two species prefer life in forests and grasslands, but they also will live close to us. A diversity of mice thrives in every climate and ecosystem on every continent on our planet, with the exception of Antarctica. If you were to study the lives of the various mouse species, you would uncover many fascinating facts and interesting stories. However, it is the house mouse that is the subject of this chapter.

The house mouse began its coexistence with humans eight thousand to ten thousand years ago on the dry grasslands of central Asia, where it lived in

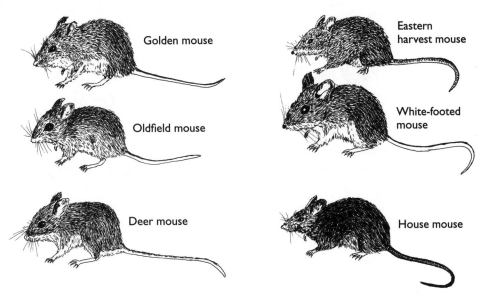

A large variety of mice can be found in different habitats.

the wild on seeds and insects. In more recent times, people began constructing granaries, barns, and sheds to store seed crops, and the house mouse started to build nests in these structures, in addition to residential dwellings. A big advantage for the mouse was that most predators would not invade these places, except perhaps for a few cats and dogs.

As the human population moved from Asia into India and throughout Europe, they unwittingly carried these house mice with them wherever they went. They even carried them across the seas to the New World aboard sailing ships from Spain, Portugal, France, and England in the 1500s. Today this two-ounce marvel is found with humankind on nearly every land mass and in nearly every ecosystem on earth, from the equator to the subpolar regions. Among all the species of mice, it is the house mouse that gets the prize for developing strategies that have allowed it to find suitable niches in so many different ecosystems. This accomplishment has been possible, in part, due to its ability to adapt to a variety of foods.

House mice have kept pace with us because they are highly adaptive mammals that quickly learn to take advantage of our food and shelter to start new colonies wherever they find themselves. There is no place too humble, no discarded food morsel too unappealing for these opportunistic little mammals. They have even been known to eat such things as paste and glue or the plastic insulation on wires.

Although house mice prefer to live in buildings, they are occasionally found outdoors, especially during the warmer months. With the coming of the cold season, they return to the warmth of our homes, garages, barns, and sheds, where they build cozy nests in dark, quiet places. Populations of house mice are relatively stable and have been known to reach a density of up to ten mice per square yard. The individual range of a house mouse—the amount of space it uses to search for food, water, and companionship—can be as little as ten square yards.

Sometimes house mice return to the wild and live independently of us. This happens when some mice are forced from the major colony due to food shortages, insufficient space, or other problems related to overpopulation. Those forced outside the colony adopt somewhat different social patterns, and they frequently find themselves in competition with established populations of wild native rodents such as deer mice and white-footed mice. In contrast to their house-loving relatives, house mouse populations living in the wild contain fewer individuals, about one per one hundred square yards. A mouse's range in such a situation can be from a few hundred to a few thousand square yards.

These feral mice eat plant leaves, stems, and seeds, as well as insects. They are found in widely diverse habitats and have been reported in such unlikely places as coral atolls, grasslands, deserts, freshwater marshes, and sand dunes. The ancestors of these wild house mice came to these places with humans.

House mice do well in every ecosystem except where they have to compete with deer mice and white-footed mice. The problem increases when these usually outdoor species seek shelter in buildings during the cold months where house mice have already established their colonies.

Another factor in the success of the house mouse has been what scientists call reproductive adaptability, which means that it can adapt its reproductive cycle to a variety of circumstances. In addition, it reproduces in extraordinary numbers in almost any situation. There are several mechanisms that make this possible.

Female house mice begin their remarkable reproduction cycle when they are very young, between forty-five and sixty days old. Even more surprising, they can produce a litter every sixteen to thirty days. Each litter contains an average of four to seven young, sometimes as many as twelve. These young mice are small versions of their parents, except for their naked pink skin and closed eyes, which remain so for about fourteen days. A mother mouse can be so overwhelmed by the sheer number of offspring that she engages the services of females from her previous litters at feeding time.

Female mice can produce more than five litters per year. During the warm months, the number of litters increases. Since each of her young becomes sexually mature in about two months, the results of this reproductive pattern are frequently prodigious, and ecological explosions sometimes occur. In one of these dramatic events in the wild, a population reached tens of thousands of mice (some reports indicated in excess of eighty thousand) on one acre of land. This kind of explosion is always cut short by natural circumstances. Food supplies are limited, predator populations increase, and even water cycles intervene. The individuals in this particular mouse explosion ate all of the available food, and most ultimately starved to death.

The prey-predator cycle is another mechanism that helps keep the number of mice in check. Typical predators are owls, hawks, snakes, foxes, cats, ferrets, wolves, raccoons, and dogs—almost any animal larger than the mouse. When the mouse population increases, their predators succeed in raising more of their offspring to maturity. Predator populations continue to increase until their food supply of mice is reduced, which in turn leads to a decline in the population of predators. The house mouse is not even safe from the sharp teeth of rats and other mice.

Their greatest protection is to stay close to the nest, and they seldom stray more than two hundred feet in any direction from safety. You may have seen a mouse scurry across your kitchen floor from one object of shelter to another. When living in the wild, this behavior is essentially the same. If necessary, they race across open areas, darting between objects that offer protection from the sky as well as from the ground. They will even swim across a small body of water to find safety, even though they don't like to get wet. They have so many enemies outdoors that house mice live for only about two or three months in those habitats. In our homes, we are their worst enemies. We set traps for them, but they often learn how to extract the bait and enjoy the snack without getting caught. We spread poison in the vicinity of a nest, but they learn to identify it and avoid it. If they are in our homes, barns, sheds, and other outbuildings, we hope that resident dogs and cats will earn their keep by reducing the mouse population. Alas, that doesn't work either. A few mice may be caught by our pets, but the colony recovers more quickly than we had hoped.

House mice are extremely territorial. Indoors, they seldom venture more than thirty feet from their nest. Each colony has an alpha mouse; he has won this rank by being victorious in battle with another male. When they are in the throes of this fight, it may appear to be a struggle that will end the life of the weaker mouse, but it seldom does. With the battle over, the alpha male chases

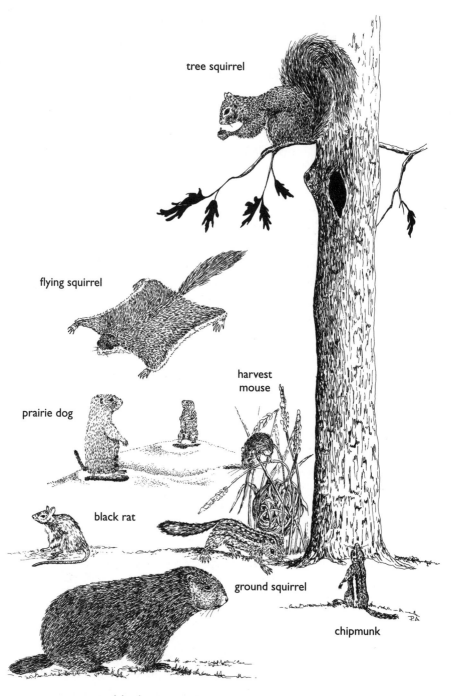

tree squirrel

flying squirrel

prairie dog

harvest mouse

black rat

ground squirrel

chipmunk

woodchuck or marmot

Mice form only a small portion of the great mammal order Rodentia.

THE ANIMALS

the loser away and proceeds to mark his hard-won territory with urine. If an outsider should amble into the territory of a marked colony, a chase always ensues.

Marking the territory not only keeps other males away, but also brings females into the male's domain. His territory, like that of other mice, can be identified by the odor of his urine, which mice can detect from as far away as seven inches. Although this is not a great distance for us, a house mouse is only a little more than three inches from the tip of its nose to the end of its body (excluding its tail).

House mice are generally nocturnal. However, they have learned to adapt to our habits. When we are away during the day, they take advantage of our absence to roam the house in search of food, and we are often surprised at where they find nourishment. Their habit of pilfering is reflected in their formal name, *Mus musculus*. *Mus* is Latin for "mouse," and *musculus* can be traced to the Sanskrit word *musha*, which means "thief."

Mice belong to the largest order of mammals, Rodentia. The order Rodentia, the rodents, has claim to the greatest number of mammal species, about 2,060, and the largest number of individuals. It includes porcupines, squirrels, chipmunks, gophers, muskrats, voles, lemmings, rats, nutrias, guinea pigs, gerbils, and hamsters, to name a few living in the United States. It also has other representatives around the world, such as chinchillas and capybaras.

Rodents are easy to identify by the type, number, and arrangement of their teeth. One characteristic of rodents is the single pair of long, chisel-like incisors located in the front of both the upper and lower jaws. These teeth are used for gnawing. The name rodent comes from the Latin word for "gnaw,"

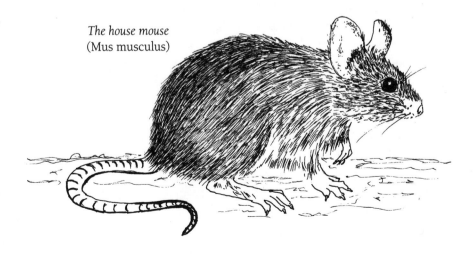

The house mouse
(Mus musculus)

which reflects the use of these prominent teeth. In mice, a wide space separates these teeth from the cheek or grinding teeth. The patterns on the cusps of these teeth distinguish one mouse species from another.

THE WORLD OF HOUSE MICE

What you will need	Science skills
basic kit	observing
live trap	comparing
hamster cage	inferring
food and water	
patience	

OBSERVATIONS

Observing wild animals is a difficult task requiring knowledge of the animal, stealth, and patience. Field biologists devote many years to the scientific observation of lions, wolves, chimpanzees, elephants, birds, lizards, sharks, and even certain insects. Amateur scientists have observed squirrels and other common animals in their natural settings without spending lots of money or traveling to far-off places. You can do this with the common house mouse if you have some basic knowledge and perseverance. Note: When handling mice, you are advised to wear latex gloves. In general, the much-maligned house mouse does little damage, and the occurrence of diseases they can carry is rare. Try some of the suggested activities with house mice, and you'll find that these tiny mammals are not as frightening as you may have thought.

Discovering Their Presence. Mice that live with us can be active at any hour of the day or night. This habit may give you the opportunity to locate a nest, although their tendency to be secretive can make sighting them difficult. You usually realize you are sheltering house mice when you find their tiny, black waste pellets in the kitchen, basement, attic, or garage. They are about the size and shape of a grain of rice.

Although not a common experience, you also may spot a wary mouse peeking out from behind an object or get a blurred glimpse of gray or brown as it streaks from one hiding place to another inside the house. No matter where the nest is located, a mouse outside of its nest is on a mission. Its goal is to find food and avoid you and other predators in the process.

Another sign that you may be harboring house mice is nesting material stashed away in a closet, on a shelf, or in a drawer. Such a nest is a loose structure put together with such things as shreds of paper, string, rags, or wool from sweaters and lined with a soft material. If you find a newly constructed nest, leave it alone. Check it every few days, and take note of any changes.

Obtaining a Mouse. You can learn a great deal about mice by observing them. Since observing mice on the loose can be difficult, you might want to try trapping one in a live trap. You can buy these nonlethal traps at hardware stores. Among the popular brands are Havahart and Victor Live Catch mousetraps. For more information, see their websites, www.havahart.com and www.victorpest.com.

If there are no signs of mice around your house, or if you have some misgivings about handling wild mice, many pet stores sell mice, which are a domesticated strain of *Mus musculus*. These mice are close relatives of the house mouse and make good pets.

A Home for Your Mouse. A hamster cage makes a good home for your mouse. They come in various sizes and are equipped with various amenities that add comfort for your pet. The hamster condo, with an exercise wheel and a plastic tube connecting two levels, is a good choice. Your mouse will also need a water bottle, which may come with the cage. If you've captured a house mouse or other wild mouse, this setup makes fine temporary housing, but you should release the mouse back into the wild when you have completed your observations.

Mouse Identification. Besides house mice, there are two additional species of mice that may find their way into your living space, especially when cold weather arrives: the white-footed mouse (*Peromyscus leucopus*) and the deer mouse (*Peromyscus maniculatus*). They belong to a group called white-footed mice, of which seventeen species live in the United States. Both of these mice have white feet and white underparts, and they look so much alike that they are often treated as one species in the popular literature. They, along with several others in the genus *Peromyscus*, are so similar in appearance that even specialists have difficulty distinguishing one from the other, especially where their ranges overlap. The house mouse can be distinguished from white-footed mice by coloring: House mice have grayish brown fur and buff or gray bellies, whereas white-footed mice have reddish brown backs and white bellies and feet.

Mouse Anatomy. With the help of a large hand lens, take a good, long look at your mouse. Spend about ten minutes. Record your observations. Was there

The deer mouse
(Peromyscus maniculatus)

anything about the mouse that surprised you? The length of the whiskers? The size of the eyes relative to the size of the head? The texture of the tail? The texture of the fur? The following questions will guide you through your observations.

Color. What color is the mouse? Is it all one color, or is it streaked? What color is the underside? Is the color uniform, or is there a hint of another color?

Texture. Is the fur soft and smooth or wiry?

Size. How long is the mouse? What is the relationship of the length of the body to the length of the head? Of the length of the body, including the head, to the length of the tail?

Legs and feet. What color are the legs and feet? Are the back and front legs the same length? Do you think the mouse is a good jumper? Describe the size difference between the front and hind feet. What advantage is there to the size of the feet?

Toes. Are the toes furry or hairless? Draw a picture that shows the location of the toes on the front and hind feet. Describe the claws. Are they long or short, dull or sharp? Are they on all the toes of the front and hind feet? What is the advantage to having such claws?

Weight. A house mouse generally weighs between one-half and one ounce. If you have a kitchen scale used for weighing food, you can use it to find out the weight of your mouse. Is it within the normal range?

Tail. Is the tail as long as or longer than the body? Is it covered with fur, completely naked, or somewhere in between? Is it scaly?

Head and snout. Describe the shape of the head and snout.

Eyes. Where on the head are the eyes located? Are they toward the front of the head, like those of a dog, or on the sides of the head, like the eyes of a bird? Do they protrude? How big are they? What color are they? Does the mouse appear to blink?

Ears. Where on the head are the ears located? How big are they relative to the head? Are the outer ears covered with fur? Is the inner surface of the ears furry or hairless? Describe their texture. Do the ears remain in one position, or does the mouse move them toward the source of a sound? Do you think the mouse can hear well?

Whiskers. Are the whiskers constantly moving, or does the mouse seem to move them only when it is exploring a new object or environment? How many delicate whiskers are there? How long are they? Are they longer or shorter than the mouse is wide?

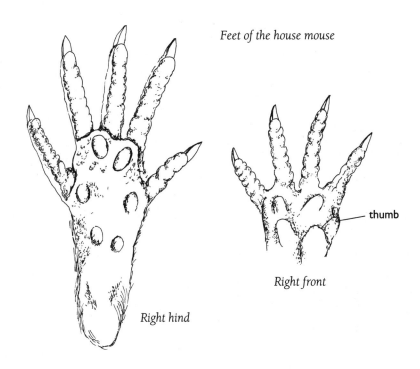

Feet of the house mouse

thumb

Right front

Right hind

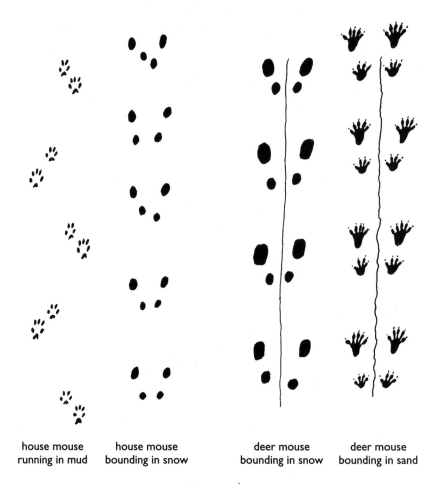

| house mouse running in mud | house mouse bounding in snow | deer mouse bounding in snow | deer mouse bounding in sand |

Mouse tracks

Grooming. Watch a mouse clean itself. Can you see a pattern to the procedure? What other mammals have you seen use a similar pattern?

Mouse Tracks. If you find a set of tiny tracks in the snow, perhaps you will be able to determine if a white-footed mouse or a deer mouse has made them. Both species hop by putting their smaller front feet down and swinging their hind feet alongside and in front of them. The tracks of deer mice may show evidence of the tail, although they frequently travel with the tail held vertically. The tail of a house mouse is always longer than the body and leaves a track that is relatively easy to see in fresh snow. Although it is rare for the house mouse to venture outside the home, its trail will look similar to that of the white-footed mouse.

EXPLORATIONS

Mouse Behavior. How does the mouse explore its surroundings? One at a time, put various objects into the mouse's cage. Some ideas are a cat toy, yarn, small twigs, a peanut in a shell, a banana, a piece of raw meat, some cheese, water with sugar, and water with salt. Record what the mouse does as it investigates each of the objects. Are there any generalizations you can make about how the mouse investigates objects introduced into its environment?

Mouse Interactions. Introduce another mouse to the cage. How does your mouse react to the presence of the other mouse? Does it retreat from the newcomer, or do they approach one another?

Mapping Mouse Movements. Field biologists study the habits of animals in the wild, such as what they eat, where they find shelter, and how far they travel during their waking hours. Since the scientists cannot observe the animals all day, every day of the year, they use a system of observing the animals for short periods of time, called sampling. You can learn about certain behaviors of your mouse through sampling. You will need a time keeper, recorder, and observer to carry out this investigation. Perhaps you can enlist the help of some friends.

First, obtain a box approximately twenty-five inches long by thirty-three inches wide by twenty-four inches high. The box must be large enough to allow the mouse to move freely, and the walls must be high enough that the mouse cannot escape. Mark the center of the box with a circle, and write the number "1" in the circle. This is the starting place for the mouse. For record keeping, use a sheet of paper the same shape as the bottom of the box. Draw a circle with this number "1" at the center of the record sheet.

Now introduce the mouse into the box by placing it on the circle. After ten seconds, draw a circle marked with a "2" on your map to indicate the new position of the mouse. Use an arrow to indicate the direction the mouse is facing. Continue noting the mouse's position in this way every ten seconds for about five minutes, numbering each new location sequentially. Then put the mouse back in its cage.

For the next trial, construct a shelter from an eight and a half-by-eleven-inch piece of cardboard, folding it to create a three-sided tent. Place it at one end of the box, and place some food at the other end. Put the mouse in the circle at the center of the box, and record its movements as you did during the first investigation, using a new record sheet. What did you discover? Were your findings what you expected? If you have more than one mouse, repeat the process with another mouse.

After several days, repeat these investigations. Are the findings the same or different? If they are different, describe the differences. Does it seem to matter if you stay well back from the observation area? Would the mouse behave differently if you went away and used a video camera mounted to view the behavior? Field scientists also have to consider how their presence might affect their observations of animal behavior.

Now analyze your record sheets. Where are the most circles placed? How many are in the corners of the box? In the center of the box? Do you see a pattern in the mouse's movements? Did the mouse tend to seek the wall of the box? The corners? The open space? Did the mouse spend much time in the shelter? (See Chapter Note.)

Did the mouse demonstrate any other behaviors? Can you study them systematically? What happens if you place one or more small boxes upside down in the test area?

CHAPTER NOTE

Although mice must leave the nest for food, to find a mate, or to explore an area for a nest site, this behavior is in conflict with their desire for cover and safety. The mice have resolved this conflict by avoiding open spaces. They follow "walls" created by logs, fallen trees, vegetation, and other objects. Animal behaviorists refer to this as "wall-seeking behavior."

CHAPTER 10

Cats

CUTE CUDDLERS AND CUNNING HUNTERS

One of the most popular musicals ever to hit the American stage has a simple, one-word title: *Cats*. At each performance, the audience is entertained by a cast of delightful, talented people dressed as *Felis catus*. But even the great popularity of this production does not match the popularity of the house cat in the hearts and homes of American people. The domestic cat "rules the roost" in about 60 million households in the United States. There may be another 60 million cats that live, like the ones depicted in the musical, by their own wits in the cities and countryside, close to people but independent.

What is this creature we call the domestic cat, this animal that has found its way into our lives and our literature, art, and music? How long has it been around, and how did it come to be?

Fossil evidence shows that mammals first appeared during the Jurassic period, some 200 million years ago. These early mammals were very small, about the size of mice, and darted about the land in the shadow of conifers and tropical palmlike plants called cycads, while birds flew overhead and the dinosaur population reached its peak. Then during the Tertiary period, 60 million years ago, dinosaurs vanished, and mammals diversified and began to dominate the animal world, along with birds and insects. Flowering plants, termed angiosperms, became the divas of the plant world.

Experts tell us that one of these early mammals was miacis, a carnivore with a long, slender body, short legs, and a long tail. Miacis was able to climb trees with the help of clawed toes. This prehistoric animal roamed the swamps and forests of its time and has been identified as the ancestor of hyenas, skunks, frogs, foxes, bears, raccoons, cats, dogs, and other mammals.

The branch holding the cat family, Felidae, appeared about 30 to 40 million years ago. An offshoot of this branch gave rise to the saber-toothed cats, huge, slow-moving yet powerful beasts that preyed on large, awkward mammals such as mammoths, elephants, and mastodons. Saber-toothed cats died out relatively recently, about twelve thousand to fifteen thousand years ago, although they persist in fictional literature. Another offshoot was the true cats, which were of medium size and were skilled at ambush killing of smaller prey. Fossil evidence indicates that about 3 million years ago, during the Pleistocene epoch (Ice Age), many mammals decreased in size, especially those in the genus *Felis,* which were among the smallest. These cats were smaller in stature than their predecessors and had correspondingly smaller skulls and brains. These size reductions were also evident in their jaws and in the number and size of their teeth. These modifications may have been the result of long-term climatic changes as ice sheets spread and then receded. Among these smaller

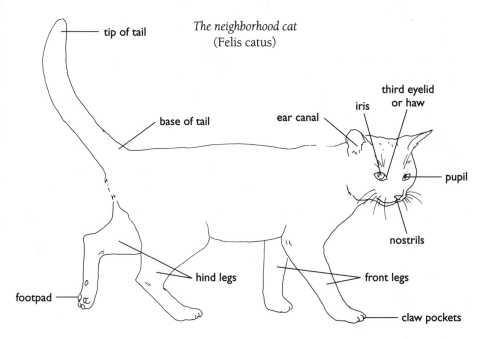

The neighborhood cat
(Felis catus)

tip of tail

base of tail

ear canal

iris

third eyelid or haw

pupil

nostrils

hind legs

front legs

footpad

claw pockets

cats, *Felis silvestris,* the European and African wildcats, appeared between nine hundred thousand and six hundred thousand years ago. These cats are believed to be the ancestors of *Felis catus,* our modern domestic cat.

From this evolutionary beginning, the cat was a solitary creature and a successful predator that earned its living in the wild. At this point, the advancing civilization of *Homo sapiens* comes into the story. The fertile flood-plains of the Nile provided the Egyptians with enough grain to store a surplus against hard times. This surplus gave them economic and political stability, but it was under constant threat from vast hordes of mice. The Egyptians enlisted the cat to save them from this threat. Over time, the cats were not only domesticated, but also became highly revered by the Egyptians, who showed their gratitude by representing them on tomb frescoes and in early paintings and statues. The esteem the Egyptians had for cats did not stop there. Cats came to be considered godlike and were often embalmed, mummified, and buried ceremoniously along with the pharaohs and the nobility.

Cats were also treasured by the Greeks and Romans. But during the Middle Ages, attitudes toward the cat disintegrated. Cats came to be thought of as symbols of evil, and anyone keeping a cat was punished by torture. For some time, the cat was no longer an object of religious worship and veneration and became something to be feared. We see vestiges of this in the

Halloween links between witches and black cats. Cats did not disappear from towns or farms, however, because, despite all the negative publicity, even an evil cat was preferable to rodents devouring the wheat, barley, and oats, leaving everyone not only hungry, but also without beer.

Since the sailing ships also needed cats to keep rodents from eating up their grain supply, cats came along to the New World with the settlers, but the negative attitudes toward them endured until the 1700s. Cats came back into favor because people needed them to control the brown rats that had again appeared on the agricultural scene and in developing food industries. Once again the cat was elevated to a better position in society, a position that many cats continue to enjoy today.

No matter how we view our domestic cats—whether they are pampered pets upon which we bestow lavish gifts of gourmet food and designer collars or simply furry companions—they often retain the solitary aloofness of the hunters of long ago.

A popular notion about the cat is that it is a completely solitary creature that prefers to live and "work" alone. This is only part of the picture, because they are not completely solitary. Wild cats wander alone during the day, but they often gather together when night falls. People who have more than one cat will attest to this with their own observations of domestic cats.

Ever since the Egyptians domesticated the wild cats of their time, there have been individual cats that have gone back to their wild state. These are known as feral cats. No matter how well cat owners care for their cats, they cannot extinguish the cats' hunting instincts. Researchers have found that the domesticated house cat is not an effective hunter, although it may occasionally catch a mouse or small bird. In fact, these cats can be quite frightened by a large, angry rat. When rats and cats are in the same area, they will ignore each other as long as the cat has found a reliable source of food. A feral cat or one kept on a farm but not fed regularly might be more likely to control the rat population.

Many cats find themselves abandoned or somehow separated from their homes and must fend for themselves. Cats with such a lifestyle are generally in poor condition. Communities of these cats often develop in urban areas, where they not only survive, but also establish territories and form communities or social groups.

A community of feral cats will not have the kind of social order that exists in a pack of wild dogs. Cats are solitary hunters, but dogs hunt in packs. Nevertheless, there is a social order or community that becomes established. This social order is not fixed, but varies with time and place. A cat that is dominant in one group at a particular time may be the inferior cat at another time. If you live in an area with a feral cat community, you may have had your sleep disturbed by their nocturnal concerts. Why these gatherings occur is not known, although it is suspected that in neutral territory, the local feral cats have declared a truce. Generally, there is no fighting during these events. In fact, if you were to observe the meetings, you would probably see the cats grooming one another. Biting and hissing rarely occur, since the gatherings are not held during the mating season. The meetings generally last until midnight, at which time each cat returns to its territory and resumes its solitary hunting life.

There have been many efforts to reduce populations of feral cats. Organizations have pooled their efforts to help reduce the number of cats living in this way. Some gather the cats, have them neutered by veterinarians, and make efforts to find homes for them.

Cats have excellent eyesight. Their vision is the primary tool used in hunting, and it is especially acute when they move around and capture prey on dark, moonless nights. Scientists tell us that the cat's daylight vision is perfect and the smallest night light is magnified forty to fifty times, providing the cat with more than adequate light to hunt successfully at night.

Cats' eyes are located forward on the face, which means they have binocular vision just as we do. This enables them to see objects in front of them as well as those at a distance. Experts believe that although cats can see objects close to them, they are not in sharp focus unless the objects are several feet away. Each eye has a range of vision of about 287 degrees. This astounding fact, coupled with the flexible neck, allows the cat to be aware of what is going on in its immediate surroundings.

A cat's eyes also signal the animal's moods. For example, if the cat sees something it likes or fears, its pupils will enlarge.

A cat's senses of hearing and smell are also acute. The funnel-shaped outer ears aid in locating the sources of sounds and can be turned to catch sounds coming from a variety of different places. The ears' internal workings allow the cat to hear sounds two octaves higher than we can, and they also can detect significantly higher sounds than a dog can hear. The high-pitched squeak of a mouse or the hard, rough sound of the tiny critter gnawing on a piece of wood is easily detected by the curious cat.

With about 200 million specialized cells, a cat's nose is a good tool for picking up minute traces of fragrances that you or I would miss. Cats are extremely good at detecting scent signals left by other cats, as well as scents left by predators or prey.

The whiskers that stick out on both sides and in front of the face extend the cat's sense of touch beyond its body. With the aid of its whiskers, a cat can estimate the width of spaces before it tries to squeeze through one that is too small.

Some researcher's believe that these whiskers also are sensitive to slight movements of air currents. This is especially important to a cat navigating in the dark. Since air is in constant motion, when a cat approaches an object, this stirs up eddies or small countercurrents that may be picked up by the extremely sensitive whiskers, allowing the cat to gracefully slip past solid objects without actually seeing them.

Whiskers are extremely important for a night hunter. Not only do they help a cat find its way in the dark, but they also help the cat direct its bite to the nape of the victim's neck, where the cat destroys the nerve connections, killing its prey.

Hooked claws are valuable tools for this hunter. The claws are also used when fighting an attacker, climbing a tree, or removing debris from its fur. When not in use, the claws on the front paws are hidden in pockets, one on each toe. When a cat is walking, lying down, or sitting, the claws are hidden. When a cat strikes out, muscles contract, pulling the claws down and out of their protective sheaths; therefore, the claws are said to be protractile. If they were retractile, the cat would have to contract muscles to keep the claws hidden.

Because of improved diet and veterinary care, the average life span of today's domestic cat is between nine and fifteen years. While some claim that pedigreed cats do not live as long as mixed breeds, there are some astonishing cats that have lived beyond all expectations. One sealpoint Siamese lived to the ripe old age of thirty-one. The chart below relates ages of cats to the equivalent human ages. Notice that cats reach the adult stage very quickly but do not continue to progress to old age so rapidly.

Age of Cat	Age of Human
1	15
2	25
4	40
7	50
10	60
15	75
20	105
30	120

Very often cat owners do not realize their cats are aging. Although a cat's eating habits may not change and it still eagerly awaits meal time, there are signs that it is getting older. Grooming is not attended to the way it had been in the past. The cat is not as supple as it once was and cannot bend its spinal cord or flex its neck as it did when younger. This hampers the cat's ability to give itself a good cleaning. Because the cat's joints are not as flexible as they once were, the aging cat may need a little help getting onto the chair that has become its favorite resting place, and it also may need help climbing stairs.

Most people will describe cats as cool and independent, in sharp contrast to dogs, which are very social animals. These dissimilar behaviors are due to the markedly different social structures in which the animals developed long ago. Being cool and aloof as adults is part of the genetic makeup of a successful solitary hunter. Some cat owners will tell you their cats are loving and affectionate; this may have come about as a result of selective breeding for specific behaviors. Humans have only been breeding cats for about five thousand years, a relatively short time compared with the dog.

THE WORLD OF CATS

What you will need	Science skills
basic kit	observing
glass jar	recording
thermometer	inferring
assorted foods	experimenting

Caution: Be sure the cats you involve in the activities in this chapter are friendly cats known to you.

OBSERVATIONS

Cat Breeds. Cats come in a wide assortment of colors, sizes, and shapes, not to mention temperaments. Some are playful, and others are aloof. Some are pedigreed, and others are not. A pedigreed cat is one that has a traceable ancestry. It has specific physical characteristics and behaviors that distinguish it from other breeds.

Following are descriptions of several breeds and their unique characteristics. How many of these breeds can you spot in your neighborhood? Watch for different cat varieties when you travel away from home. You may want to ask a veterinarian or contact a local cat association for some help with your search (see Chapter Note 1). Books at your local library may aid you in identification. A camera would be helpful to get a record of a breed that you do not recognize immediately.

Abyssinian. This is a medium-sized short-haired cat that can be brown, black, or ruddy. It has a long, lithe body, large ears, and a long tail. With its slender, graceful attitude, it reminds some of a miniature version of a small wildcat, such as the cougar. It also resembles the cats of ancient Egyptian art.

American shorthair. Many house cats are American shorthairs. This is probably the most familiar kind of cat. Its ancestors were the cats that arrived on our shores with the first settlers. A fairly heavy build, heavy shoulders, broad chest, and short, heavily textured fur are its hallmarks. These cats are very affectionate, easily trained, and come in a wide variety of colors and patterns. They have the reputation of being working cats, happily patrolling barns, homes, and warehouses for rodents, which has been their job ever since they arrived with the early settlers.

Cornish rex. The high-pitched voice of the Cornish rex, although not as piercing as the voice of a Siamese, sets it apart from other cats, as do the close-lying curls on its short hair. On closer inspection, you will see curly whiskers and eyebrows as well. They have large, conspicuous ears that some characterize as flared. They are very affectionate and make good family pets. Developed in England in 1950, they arrived in the United States the following decade.

Himalayan. This relatively new breed, a cross between the short-haired Siamese and the long-haired Persian, can be distinguished by its exquisite blue eyes and its long coat, which requires regular brushing. This is a good-natured cat that can endure playful dogs and avoids squabbles with other cats. It is a good family cat.

Maine coon cat. This lovable, rugged cat needs room to roam. It loves the outdoors and can endure harsh climates. Its bushy coat and flowing fur on a long, tapering tail require little maintenance. It has a stocky, muscular build, weighing twelve to eighteen pounds, with a broad chest and large, round tufted paws. Its ancestors are thought to have been ratters on early ships to the New World.

Manx. This cat without a tail is said to have features in common with the rabbit, such as very high hind legs coupled with a typical rabbit gait. However, it is quite unlike a rabbit in its ability to climb. The manx is an intelligent, lively, and affectionate cat that makes a wonderful pet. It is also an exceptional and courageous hunter and fisher.

Persian. This breed arrived in Europe four hundred years ago from Persia, known today as Iran. This quiet, well-mannered cat makes a good photographer's model, as it is willing to sit and pose. With its stocky body and short, sturdy legs, it is heavier than many other breeds and is therefore less active. Characteristic of the Persian cat is a long, flowing coat with a ruff, a fringe of long hairs growing around the neck. The Persian has small ears, large eyes, and a fluffy tail. It has enjoyed many years of popularity.

Scottish fold. This car's ears lie flat against its head, and it is this characteristic that gives the Scottish fold its name and immediately sets it apart from other cats. In 1961, this natural mutation was found on a farm in Scotland. It has big, round eyes and enjoys the reputation of being a good family cat.

Siamese. This is a sleek, muscular, and elegant cat with a long, tapered, whiplike tail and almond-shaped eyes. Its coat is short and close fitting. A Siamese cat hates to be alone, but it usually singles out one person in a household to receive its devotion. It is very talkative. Although it appears exotic and mysterious, it loves to learn tricks. It is the only domestic cat with non-retractable claws.

Body Types. A cat will illustrate one of three body types. The *lithe* body type is seen in Siamese and Abyssinian cats. These are slender, lightly built cats with long bodies, slim legs, narrow shoulders and rump, and wedge-shaped heads.

The *cobby* cat has a stocky body, broad shoulders and rump, short, stubby legs, and a flat face. Persian cats have this body type.

The *semi-foreign* body type is represented by the American shorthair cat and Devon rex. These cats have a sturdy muscular build, intermediate leg length, medium rump and shoulder width, and slightly rounded heads.

Keep a record of the different body types you see in your neighborhood. Which type do you see most often?

Flexible Body. You need only observe a cat for a short time to realize that its body is extremely flexible, an advantage in the many activities a cat engages in during a day. You can see this flexibility at work when a cat is stalking prey,

You can see the flexibility of the cat's body when it is stalking prey.

stretching after a nap, or arching its back when frightened. With a supple neck, the cat is able to look over its shoulder and to give its rump a wash.

The flexible body also works to the cat's advantage when running. Unlike the dog, a cat does not move its legs faster to obtain greater speed. Instead, the cat stretches its flexible body so that each stride covers more ground. This is an energy-saving adaptation that has worked well for both the domestic cat and its wild cousins. The cat is a sprinter, whereas the dog is a long-distance runner.

Cat Hygiene. Watch a cat grooming itself (see Chapter Note 2). Besides using its rough tongue as a washcloth, a cat may use its teeth to extract particles of dirt lodged in its fur. A very flexible spinal cord makes it possible for the cat to twist and reach almost all of its body; however, the cat cannot lick its face. How does it solve this problem? Keep a record of the steps the cat takes in cleaning itself. Is the process rather haphazard, or is there a pattern to it? Where does it begin? How does it proceed? Does the cat always follow the same pattern?

Eye Color. Cats' eyes come in a variety of colors, including gold, blue, green, copper, and amber. You will also find these colors in a variety of shades. Look at the eyes of different cats, and record the color, along with the breed, if you know it. The more cats you observe, the greater will be your appreciation for the wide range of eye colors. Keep track of how many you see with each eye color. Which color or colors appeared most frequently? Did some of the colors appear especially bright or vivid?

Third Eyelid. The cat has a third eyelid called a haw, or nictitating membrane, in the corner of each eye. If a cat needs to protect or lubricate its eyes, the haw moves across the surface of each eye, spreading tears over the cornea. If you spend some time observing your cat, you may see this membrane at work. In humans, the tiny pink lump in the corner of each eye was once a third eyelid, but it no longer functions.

Ears. Spend some time watching a cat as it lies quietly. Does it move its ears? Can you hear the sound the cat may be responding to? Cats' outer ears are not only valuable as hunting tools, but they also can express the cat's moods. For example, a happy cat perks its ears forward, whereas an angry cat lays its ears back on its head.

Nose. Cats have what is called nose leather, a patch of hairless skin around each nostril. These patches come in a variety of colors, such as black, brown, brick red, rose, pink, lavender, or blue. Look at the noses of several cats. Make a list of the different colors you see. How many times does each color appear? Keep a record of the colors you find, as well as the breeds

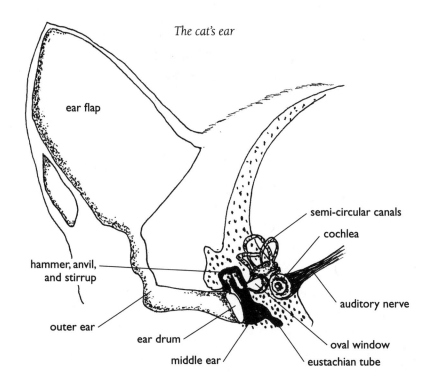

The cat's ear

ear flap

semi-circular canals

cochlea

hammer, anvil, and stirrup

auditory nerve

outer ear

ear drum

oval window

middle ear

eustachian tube

of the cats, if you know them. Are specific colors connected with specific breeds?

Feel the cat's nose. Write a description of it in your notebook.

You can watch the cat's nose at work by offering it a favorite treat in a bowl. How does the cat approach the treat?

Whiskers. Cat whiskers are specialized hairs above the lips that are designed as feelers. Gently touch the whiskers of a cat. How do they differ

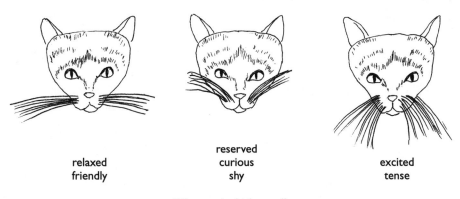

relaxed
friendly

reserved
curious
shy

excited
tense

What cats' whiskers tell us

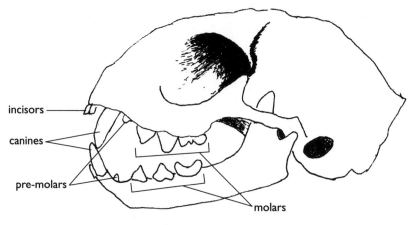

The cat's skull

from the hairs on the cat's body? How many whiskers does the cat have? Is this the same number as on other cats? How far do they extend beyond the cat's head? In what directions can the cat move them? Forward? Backward? Can the top two rows move independently of the bottom two rows? How does the cat react if you touch its whiskers?

Teeth. What kind of teeth does a cat have? To explore this question, you must have a very friendly cat. *Do not* try to examine the mouth of a strange cat or one that is not extremely friendly to you.

Cats have thirty teeth. Of these, four slightly inwardly curved canines are used for killing prey. When a cat has a firm hold on its prey, its canines bite the spinal nerves located in the nape of the prey's neck. The cat always delivers the fatal bite to the same place, regardless of the size of the prey.

Sometimes cat owners will hear their cat's teeth chattering. This is an extreme behavior associated with the killing of prey. The cat is acting as though it already has the prey in its grasp. Teeth chattering does not always need the stimulus of a mouse strolling along the grass or a bird eating seed at a feeder. It can happen without any apparent reason, at least from our point of view.

Tail. The cat's flexible tail (see Chapter Note 3) is a tool for expression. If the tail is moving in a quick, jerky manner, this shows that the cat is excited. If its tail is still and arched over its back, the cat is offering a signal of friendship. A slightly irritated cat will hold its tail still, but you will see the tip twitching. If the cat holds its tail low and fluffed, it's frightened. If the tail is straight out from the body and the hairs are stiff, this signals aggression.

THE ANIMALS

There are many more subtle signals cats give to express their moods. How many different moods can you observe in your cat? How does the cat express them with its tail? What is the cat's tail signal when it greets you? How does your cat hold its tail when it is in the presence of a dominant cat?

The cat can also use its tail to help maintain its balance as it runs along the top of a fence or leaps from one perch to another. This is similar to the way the squirrel uses its tail to maintain balance as it leaps from tree to tree. Observe the tail as a cat is jumping or balancing, and describe what it does in your notebook.

Fur. The natural coat of a cat is made up of three different types of hair: guard, awn, and down. The guard hair is straight and relatively coarse. The awn hair is a fine secondary hair, while the down hair, also a secondary hair, is soft.

These fur types work together to protect the cat from extremes in weather and temperature. Maine coon cats and the Norwegian forest cat are two breeds that have adapted to northern climates. Siamese cats lack down fur and are not well-suited for wandering outdoors in the winter. With the help of a hand lens, examine the fur on your cat. How many different kinds of fur do you find? How do they differ? What is the length of each different type of hair? Are they straight or curly? Do individual hairs have one or more colors? Observe a cat's fur in summer and in winter. How is it different? What happens to the fur when summer comes?

A cat's hair also communicates its moods. When the cat is afraid, the hair all over the body stands on end. However, if only a ridge of hair is standing on end along the cat's spine and tail, look out—this is an angry cat.

Cat Sounds. Cats are vocal creatures. They have a wide range of sounds to express anger, likes, dislikes, complaints, and delight. Listen for the sounds your cat makes over a period of a few weeks. Do you hear a meow, hiss, growl, screech, purr, or nighttime caterwauling? Keep a record of each sound, and make note of the behavior or body language the cat exhibits at that time. What conclusions can you draw about the vocalizations and the cat's moods?

Paws and Claws. Cats, unlike dogs, do not make much noise as they walk. What is it about a cat's paws that allows it to walk so quietly? Watch a cat closely as it walks. Does it walk on its toes or on the entire foot?

Examine one of the front paws of a friendly cat. Draw a picture of what you see. How many leathery pads are on the underside? What is the relationship between the pads and the claws? Where is the largest pad located? Do you think it has any effect on the cat's ability to walk noiselessly? What else

The cat keeps its front claws retracted into their skin pockets when it walks or runs. Therefore, they are always needle-sharp.

do you see that would contribute to the cat's silent gait? Now examine one of the hind feet. How does it compare with the front paws?

Compare the claws on a hind foot with those on a front foot. What differences do you notice? Are the claws equally sharp on both feet? How do you explain any difference you observe? When the cat is relaxed, press on its toes. What happens to the claws?

Scent Signals. Scent glands are another tool cats have for communicating with each other. Every cat is able to deposit an odor unique to the individual from glands located in its cheeks and near its anus. Research has not been able to determine the exact role these chemicals play in the life of a cat.

When greeting, cats will rub against each other, a behavior that deposits scents from one cat to the other. Cats will also rub against objects such as

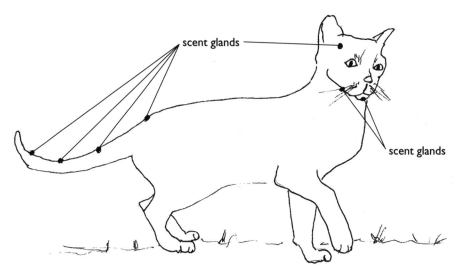

Cats possess multiple scent glands that produce a specialized, personalized odor that we can't detect.

bushes, fence posts, fire hydrants, or furniture to spread their scent. When a cat rubs against you, is this really a sign of affection, as most people assume, or is the cat marking you with its scent?

EXPLORATIONS

Eating Habits. Compare the eating habits of the cat with those of a dog. Does the cat gobble its food the way a dog does? Does either animal clean the bowl or leave some for a snack later in the day? What does each of the animals do if there is food it doesn't like? Design and carry out an investigation that will help you find out what foods your cat prefers. Feed the cat at the same time in the same place every day, use the same bowl each time, and feed it the same amount of each test food. There is a common notion that cats like milk. Find out if this old saw carries any weight with your cat.

Pupil Dilation. Our pupils react to changes in the amount of light in our environment. When we are in dim light, our pupils become larger, but in bright light, they become smaller. Do cats' pupils respond the same way? Cats' eyes react to dimming light before sunrise and after evening twilight. In a dimly lit room, shine a flashlight at the eyes of a cat, and you will see the pupils change from large and round to a narrow slit. These adaptations help the cat see in various light intensities. Cats' eyes also exhibit eyeshine, discussed in the chapter on dogs.

Staring. A cat can look at something for a very long time without blinking. Use a watch with a second hand or a stopwatch to time a cat as it stares at an object. How long does it go without blinking? Have a friend stare at something as long as he or she can without blinking. Compare the stare times of the cat and your friend. What did you find out? Try this with other cats and other people. Are the results similar or different?

Reactions to Reflections. How does a cat respond when you hold it in front of a mirror where it can see its image? Compare the reactions of the cat

pupil in darkness

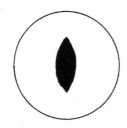

pupil in medium bright light

pupil in bright sunlight

The effect of light on a cat's pupil

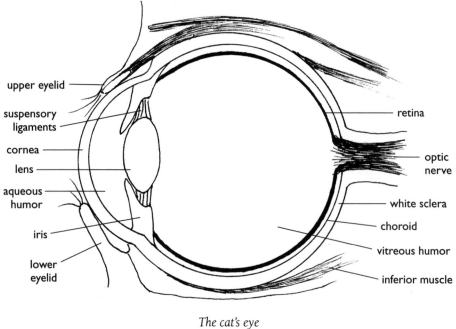

upper eyelid

suspensory ligaments

cornea

lens

aqueous humor

iris

lower eyelid

retina

optic nerve

white sclera

choroid

vitreous humor

inferior muscle

The cat's eye

with those of a dog of a similar age. What did you find out? Record the various behaviors in your notebook.

Right-Pawed or Left-Pawed. Many investigators have wondered whether a cat favors one paw over the other and have devised investigations to answer this interesting question. To determine whether your cat favors its right or left paw, put some food that your cat especially likes into a clean wide-mouthed jar. Place the open jar on its side on the floor. Be sure the food is close enough to the opening that the cat can reach it with a paw. Which paw does the cat use to scoop out the food? Try this several times. Keep a record of which paw the cat uses each time it retrieves the food. Does it always use the same paw? What did you discover?

Gait. Watch a cat as it walks. Giraffes can move the front and back legs on the same side of the body at the same time. Does your cat do this? Do the feet on the left or right side move together, or do the feet alternate from one side to the other?

You may not notice that the cat's four feet almost step in each other's tracks. A cat can walk on a path that is only two inches wide. How is this an advantage for the cat?

CHAPTER NOTES

1.   There are many organizations that encourage breeding regulations and organize cat shows. The parent of these organizations is the Cat Fanciers Association (CFA), which has many affiliates in the United States and Canada.

2. Grooming does more than clean fur. It also stimulates oil glands in the skin to produce waterproofing oils. These oils contain a substance that sunlight converts into vitamin D, which the cat swallows when it washes itself. During the summer months, licking has another advantage. The wet fur acts as a substitute for sweating. As the saliva evaporates, the cat's body is cooled in the way that our bodies are cooled by the evaporation of perspiration.

3. The flexibility of a cat's tail is due to its structure. It may have as many as twenty-eight vertebrae or as few as eighteen, but the average range is between twenty-one and twenty-three. The vertebrae decrease in size toward the tip. You can feel the vertebrae decrease in size, but you may not be able to tell that the last vertebra is caplike. Some breeds, such as the American bobtail and the manx, have significantly fewer vertebrae. In fact, the manx is often regarded as a tailless cat.

CHAPTER 11

Dogs

FAITHFUL FRIENDS

When Europeans followed Columbus to the New World, they found that the native peoples lived with domestic dogs, and that the myths and legends of these peoples, from the Aztecs in the south to the Eskimos in the far north, were filled with dog stories. This was not a unique phenomenon; dog stories also filled the lore of Egyptian, Greco-Roman, Mesopotamian, African, Asian, and Polynesian cultures. It would seem that dogs and humans have lived together all over our planet since before the dawn of civilization. This is an amazing fact and a puzzle for science.

Domestic dogs come in a wide variety of sizes and shapes, from the huge, sleek Great Dane to the cuddly little bichon frise. Some look like wolves, some look like foxes, and some resemble jackals or hyenas. Are dogs just tame versions of these wild animals? All of these animals are canids (family Canidae), grouped together because they are meat-eating carnivores that share a common tooth pattern. Scientists have long wondered whether the domestic dog had many ancestors, only a few, or just one, such as the wolf, fox, jackal, or dingo.

Stanley Coren, an animal behaviorist at the University of British Columbia, has created a "family tree" in which he shows the possible lineage of the domestic dog as well as other canids. The information for this tree was derived from evidence gathered by paleontologists. It illustrates that all canids can be traced back to a common ancestor, and that the domestic dog, through tomarctus, a wolflike animal, shares ancestry with all other canids, including coyotes, wolves, foxes, and jackals. It is interesting to note that all of these animals can and do interbreed.

In recent years, archeologists unearthed doglike bones in human burial sites and speculated that early dogs joined human groups when they first settled into stable colonies and began farming. Analysis of those bones indicated an association with humans as long ago as 14,000 years. However, DNA has since provided us with new information.

Evolutionary biologists at the University of California–Los Angeles have been studying canids' mitochondrial DNA, which is inherited only from the mother and is a reasonably accurate way to trace the ancestry of domestic dogs living today. The scientists extracted and analyzed the DNA from over 140 dogs from 67 different breeds, as well as that from wolves, coyotes, and jackals. These studies indicate that the gene sequences of domestic dogs and wolves are separated by only 1 to 2 percent, whereas wolves and coyotes differ by as much as 7.5 percent, and that wolves and coyotes separated from each other about 1 million years ago. Further analysis of the dogs' DNA indicates

Many authorities believe that the domestic dog is descended from the wolf.

that it is very variable among different breeds of dogs, which suggests that the domestic dog has been around much longer that the 14,000 years previously thought. Armed with this new information, the research team suggested that the wolf and dog separated about 135,000 years ago. The investigators also studied the gene sequence from nuclear DNA, which yielded results that also favored the wolf as the ancestor of the domestic dog.

Where the dog originated is still an unanswered question. Dogs may have evolved from different wolf populations in different parts of the world at different times. Although many scientists continue to search for answers, the evidence presently indicates that the line of descent from the wolf did not occur as a single event.

Over time, the ancestors of the domestic dog experienced some basic changes, including a reduction in the shape and size of the skull, teeth, and brain. Nevertheless, the dog still has the keen senses that enabled its ancestors to survive in the wild. One of these is the sense of smell. You only have to take a dog for a brief walk to see how he uses this sense, which has remained finely tuned through the ages. If you let him run freely in an open field, you will see him working his sense of smell. The path he weaves zigzags through the grass, crosses back on itself, and veers off in many new directions as the dog learns what has been happening in that field over a period of time.

How does the dog know where to go, where not to go, where a supply of food might be hiding, and where danger lurks? How does the dog distinguish between a bowl of meat and a bowl of fruit when he is offered both? A look at the anatomy and physiology of the dog's nose reveals some fascinating insights into this remarkable data-gathering device.

The nasal passage of the dog has over 200 million scent receptors, compared with our meager 5 million. These scent receptors are found on an elaborately folded membrane that lines the dog's nose. If this membrane were to be laid out flat, the total surface area would be greater than that of the dog's entire body.

When a dog breathes, air is transported into its respiratory system. But when a dog sniffs, the air takes an entirely different path. Sniffed air does not travel into the lungs, as breathed air does. Instead, it gets trapped in the folds in the lining of the nasal membrane, which lies over a bony shelf. When a dog breathes out, the shelf prevents the air above it from being exhaled as well. Thus molecules of sniffed air remain and accumulate. These odor molecules are quickly dissolved and adhere to receptor cells of the mucous membrane. The odor-drenched mucus on the receptor cells produces a chemical signal that is converted to an electrical signal and transferred to the emotional center of the dog's brain, where it is stored for later use.

In addition to the complex internal structure of the dog's nose that makes it highly sensitive to odors, the external portion also plays an important role in

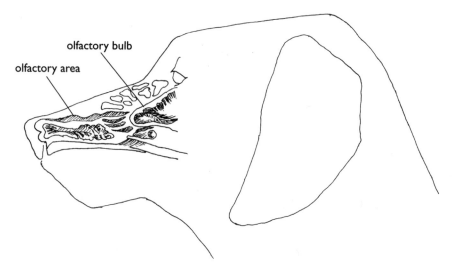

Cross section of a dog's nose

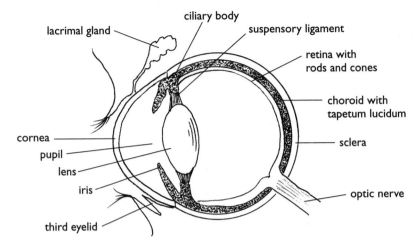

Diagram of a dog's eye

smelling. On a healthy dog, the tip of the nose is always damp. Without this moisture, a dog would not be able to grab the particles of odors that float in the air and pass them on to his internal mucous membranes.

Dogs of different breeds do not have the same degree of sensitivity to odors. Bloodhounds and beagles are extremely sensitive to ground scents and serve us well in finding missing persons and objects. German shepherds are used to sniff out drugs and explosives and even to find people buried after earthquakes and other kinds of disasters.

The dog's sense of sight is also remarkable. Although it is commonly believed that dogs see a black-and-white world, there is still speculation on whether they can discriminate among various colors. Dogs see better at night than we do, and their best vision is during the twilight hours—before dawn and after the sun sets. The reason for this is that behind the light-receptor cells of the retina, the rods and cones, is a reflective layer called the tapetum lucidum. Light coming into the eye passes through the retina and is reflected back through the tapetum lucidum. This reflection lets the dog make the most use of available light.

Like the cat, the dog has a third eyelid, or nictitating membrane, which lies beneath the lower lid. This transparent shield protects the dog's eyes from dust and other particles. This membrane is similar to that found in the eyes of birds and functions in essentially the same way.

Dogs are predators, and their eyes are in front and not on the sides of the head, as in most birds. This placement allows both eyes to look at the same object at the same time. This is called binocular vision, and it provides depth

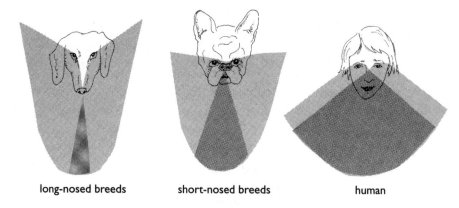

long-nosed breeds   short-nosed breeds   human

The variation in the shape of dogs' heads causes differences in eye placement and thus influences their fields of vision.

of field, the ability to focus simultaneously on objects that are near and far. Binocular vision is very important in the process of judging distance.

When humans look straight ahead, we also can see parts of objects beside us with our peripheral vision. This gives us a wide field of vision. The field of vision varies among dog breeds, from wide like ours to extremely narrow. Each of these extremes has its advantages and disadvantages. If a dog's lateral vision is exceptionally good, he will not be able to see objects directly in front of him. Afghans, poodles, and salukis would not have this difficulty, because their eyes are frontally placed, whereas those of German shepherds are more laterally placed, a design that gives them a wide field of vision and makes them effective guard dogs. Wolves' vision is more lateral than that of many breeds of dogs.

Like their wolf relatives, dogs are able to hear high-pitched sounds that are inaudible to us. This is certainly an advantage for those that feed on field mice, voles, and other small mammals, whose squeaks make these tiny prey easy to locate. Some dogs can even hear the extremely high-pitched, ultrasonic noises made by bats. Dogs also can move their ear flaps to pinpoint the location of sounds that we may or may not hear.

Humans' relationship with dogs has a long history. From the time they first joined our societies, their supersensitive senses of smell, hearing, and vision have helped us in hunting for food and gathering livestock. They have warned us and challenged predators that tried to invade our living space. Dogs that combine special personality traits and physical qualities have become invaluable guides for the blind. Therapy dogs have become an integral part of the treatments for those confined to nursing homes and convalescent centers. Some breeds, such as the Newfoundland and Portuguese water dog, are remarkable rescue dogs that save people from a variety of disastrous experiences. Other breeds are extremely helpful to law enforcement officials in their search for missing persons and in ferreting out illegal drugs and stolen goods. There is no other species that we have invited into our homes, share our food with, and have encouraged to be our companions the way we have done with dogs, animals that are unmatched in their helpfulness and devotion to us. When we take an honest look at the ledger, its easy to see which of us got the best deal in this relationship.

THE WORLD OF DOGS

What you will need

basic kit

Science skills

observing

recording

inferring

Caution: Be sure that the dogs you involve in the activities in this chapter are friendly ones known to you.

OBSERVATIONS

Identifying Dogs by Class. The early dogs looked very different from the dogs of today, although German shepherds and some other breeds do resemble the wolves from which they descended. Today we find many different breeds of dogs, such as collie, dachshund, golden retriever, Pomeranian, Labrador retriever, and poodle, to name just a few.

A breed is defined by the American Kennel Club (AKC) as a group of animals bred by humans to possess certain inheritable qualities, including a uniform appearance, that distinguish it from other members of the same species. Today the AKC divides American breeds into seven different classes, based on various roles dogs play in our lives. If you consult other sources, such as field guides to dogs, you may find some variations to this classification.

Sporting dogs. Alert and active, these dogs are selected for hunting. Members of this group include spaniels, setters, and pointers.

Terriers. These are high-energy dogs, often described as feisty. Airedales, cairn terriers, Welsh terriers, and West Highland white terriers are a few representative breeds.

Hounds. An acute sense of smell has led to the nickname "scenthounds" for some members of the group. Others are prized for their vision and are called "sighthounds." Beagles, bloodhounds, dachshunds, and whippets are in this group.

Working dogs. These dogs serve us by guarding property, pulling sleds, or rescuing people. Newfoundlands, Portuguese water dogs, Bernese mountain dogs, boxers, and Doberman pinschers are among the working dogs.

Herding dogs. Formerly grouped with the working dogs, these specialized dogs came into their own in 1983. They are known for their ability to herd other animals, including humans, controlling their movements. Run along with one of these dogs, and you will find yourself gently brought to a standstill. The size of herd animals is unimportant. The dogs do the job as well with cows as they do with ducks. Shetland sheepdogs, border collies, Pembroke Welsh corgis, and collies are in this group.

Toy dogs. These small dogs are often called lap dogs. Their small size contrasts sharply with their effectiveness as watchdogs. Members of this group are toy poodles, miniature pinschers, Chihuahuas, and Italian greyhounds.

Non-sporting dogs. The poodle, Lhasa apso, Boston terrier, bulldog, and shih tzu are members of this group. Many of us have wonderful dogs that are not members of any AKC classification. These mixed-breed dogs are "special blends," and perhaps they deserve a category of their own.

Can you determine what category your dog or the dog you're observing falls into?

Eyes. Examine the eyes of a friendly dog. Depending on the dog's breed, his eyes may be round, oval, almond, or triangular. What shape are they?

	almond	Great Pyrenees, West Highland white terrier, Siberian husky, German shepherd
	oval	poodle, miniature schnauzer, schipperke
	round	French bulldog, bichon frise, Boston terrier, Pekingese
	triangular	bull terrier, Akita, Afghan hound (almost triangular)

Eye shapes of different breeds

Make a chart of the various types of dog eyes you find in your neighborhood.

Eye Type	Breed	Number Observed
oval		
round		
almond		
triangular		

The eyes of many varieties of wolves are oval and slightly oblique, those of most foxes are linear or slit-shaped, and those of jackals are round.

What color is the iris? If you or a friend has a puppy, observe the eyes as the puppy grows older. How old is the dog when the color changes? Look at the eyes of adult dogs of several different breeds. Does the color of the iris vary?

Ears. The external flap, or pinna, is the readily visible portion of the dog's external ear, and it varies in shape and texture depending on the breed. Beneath the external hair, skin, and muscle is an underlying support of cartilage. Watch a dog listen to the sounds in the environment, and you will see the effect of the muscles at work while you witness the amazing mobility of dogs' ears. Observe the dog for about twenty minutes. How often did your dog move his ears? How do the ears move? How much do they twist and turn? What are the advantages of this mobility? Could you hear any sounds in the environment when your dog moved his ears?

Look past the flap into the ear. What shape is the canal? Is it like a funnel, or is it more like a tube? How does the shape of the canal help the dog hear? Take a sheet of paper and roll it into a funnel. Hold the small end of the funnel up to your ear. How does this affect your hearing?

As you observe a variety of dogs in your neighborhood, you will notice that the design of the external flap varies from one dog to another. The differences may be in the length or width of the flap, or you may see a variety of shapes. Many dogs are born with floppy external flaps, but sometimes the owners of certain breeds have cosmetic surgery done on their dogs so that they will conform to a breed standard. This changes a hanging or folded ear into an upright ear. Some of the breeds that traditionally have undergone this minor cosmetic surgery are Doberman pinschers, boxers, schnauzers, and Boston terriers. Make a chart of the various types of dog ears you find in your neighborhood.

Ear Type	Breed	Number Observed
erect		
semierect		
folded		
batlike		
long		
short		

Communication. Dogs are marvelous transmitters of information, and one way they do this is through facial expressions. Happy expressions of the dog include an open mouth, ears directed forward, and a tongue that hangs loosely. A dog displays anxiety with lips drawn way back and ears flattened against its head, usually accompanied by a whine. Visual signs of a threat may include a wrinkled nose, lips pulled forward to display teeth, and erect

The threat display in a dog is characterized by these signs: a wrinkled nose, open mouth with teeth bared, ears erect, and a forward-pointing and erect tail.

THE ANIMALS

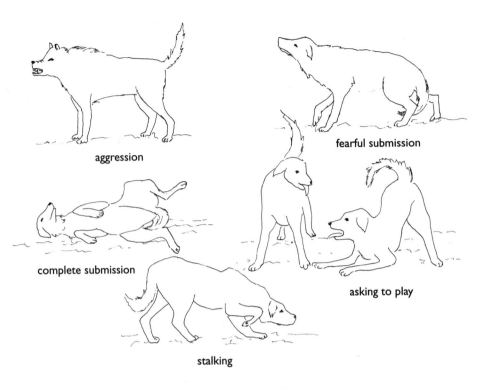

aggression

fearful submission

complete submission

asking to play

stalking

What dogs' bodies tell us

ears. Growls or snarls often accompany these visual signs. A raised tail is another declaration that all is not well.

The way a dog carries its tail and what it does with that tail also tell a lot about what is going on in the dog's mind. When in a playful mood, a dog will wag its tail vigorously. In the position of dominant aggression, the dog will hold its tail and ears upright while it snarls and shows its teeth. Another aggressive pose is that of fearful aggression, in which the tail is held out and rigid, the ears are laid back, the lips are curled, and the teeth are bared. If you should see a dog in either of these poses, stay away from it. It may be frightened or feel threatened and is probably getting ready to attack.

Tails. A purebred dog has a type of tail that is distinctive of the breed, but dogs that are mixed breeds demonstrate characteristic tails as well. Look in your neighborhood for the different tail types that appear in the following illustrations.

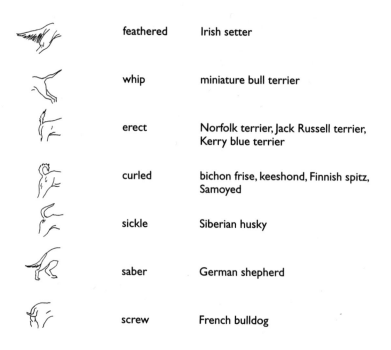

	feathered	Irish setter
	whip	miniature bull terrier
	erect	Norfolk terrier, Jack Russell terrier, Kerry blue terrier
	curled	bichon frise, keeshond, Finnish spitz, Samoyed
	sickle	Siberian husky
	saber	German shepherd
	screw	French bulldog

Tail types of different breeds

Make a chart listing the tail varieties you observe.

Tail Type	Breed	Number Observed
feathered		
whip		
erect		
curled		
sickle		
saber		
screw		

You may have noticed squirrels using their tails as balancing aids when they hop from limb to limb and from tree to tree. Look for dogs using their tails in a similar way when they jump over fences and other obstacles.

Comparing Dog and Cat Feet. Examine the feet of a few friendly dogs and cats. What similarities and differences do you observe? Which group of animals has more heavily padded feet? How do the claws of the cat and dog differ? Are both animals able to withdraw their claws?

Dominance versus Submission. Even though dogs don't travel in packs, they do illustrate dominance and submission through play. In a frequent display of these roles, one dog will roll over on its back while the other dog engages in playful biting. What happens if the standing dog bites too hard? How does the submissive dog let the other know it has gone too far?

What happens when two female dogs or two male dogs of about the same age play? Does one show dominance over the other? If both dogs are the

Cats have round tracks (left) with no claws showing at the tips of their toe pads. Dogs' hind feet (right) usually land a little to the side or behind the front feet.

Dogs show submissiveness by such actions as grovelling with their head and tail down, crawling on their belly, and trying to lick the lips of the dominant dog.

same age but one is female and the other male, which dog demonstrates dominance? Do these dogs always assume the same roles?

Can you think of other behaviors that illustrate dominance and submission in dogs? (See Chapter Note 1.)

EXPLORATIONS

Learned versus Inherited Behavior. There are basically two types of dog behavior. One kind is genetically inherited, such as the need to satisfy hunger, and the other is learned. Dogs that have been trained to come on command are displaying learned behavior. Observe your dog carefully for about a week, and make a list of those behaviors that are inherited and those that are learned.

Go to a wide-open space, such as a field or park, and stand at one end of the field without your dog knowing you are there. Have a friend blindfold your dog and take him about a hundred yards away, then remove the blindfold. Wave to your dog, but don't call his name. How does he respond? Call the dog's name. Does his response change? Does he show learned behavior by responding to your call, or does he simply ignore your voice and illustrate instinctive behavior by smelling the grass in the vicinity of your friend?

Field of Vision. Sheepdogs (herding dogs) have a 180-degree field of vision. The field of vision for the Pekingese is 5 to 10 degrees, and that of terriers is

20 to 30 degrees. Design an investigation that will give you some idea of your dog's field of vision.

Eyeshine. Unlike our eyes, those of the dog are designed to help it see best in dim light. In a dark room, shine a flashlight into your dog's eyes. What color do you see? How do you explain the color? (See Chapter Note 2.)

Sense of Smell. Observe your dog breathing normally when at rest. How would you describe its breathing? Time the number of respirations in a minute. How does that compare with your own number of respirations in a minute?

What happens to the dog's breathing when you introduce a new, unexpected odor, such as perfume on a piece of cloth? Observe the dog's behavior. What does he do with his nose? This behavior is called sniffing. How does it differ from the ordinary breathing you observed?

Smell versus Taste. Experts tell us that the dog's sense of smell is far superior to its sense of taste. Offer your dog a piece of food. What is the first thing the dog does when offered the food? Does the dog taste your offering immediately, or does he sniff the food first?

CHAPTER NOTES

1. Young dogs and females may engage in submissive urination when approached by an owner or a dominant dog. In the wild this behavior is used by timid dogs to diffuse aggression on the part of the dominant dog in the pack. This behavior causes trouble in a home when a submissive dog is punished for the act, as it only strengthens the reaction in the non-aggressive dog. It is helpful to think of submission as a normal reaction on the part of a dog. It is a way of preventing attack by a dominant being, either an aggressive dog or a human being.

An aggressive dog will try to assert dominance over its owner by a growl or a snap when an owner tries to put them outdoors, groom them, or move them from a chair. These behaviors occur if the owner is not seen by the dog as a strong "leader of the pack."

There are many factors that can cause dominant or submissive behavior in a dog. Genetics plays a large role in determining the extent to which a dog will illustrate these behaviors. The environment in which a dog lives is another determining factor. For example, if the father is a person who yells orders at other family members, a dog living in that environment may demonstrate submissive behavior, especially if it is genetically predisposed to do so.

2. If you shine the beam of a flashlight at a dog's eyes, the light you see in the eyes is the result of light reflecting off the tapetum lucidum and is called eyeshine. You may have seen this phenomenon when the headlights of your car caught the eyes of a raccoon, opossum, or other nocturnal animal.

SELECTED BIBLIOGRAPHY

Borror, Donald, and Richard E. White. *A Field Guide to the Insects.* Boston: Houghton Mifflin, 1970.

Burt, William H., and Richard P. Grossenheider. *A Field Guide to the Mammals.* Boston: Houghton Mifflin, 1976.

Cobb, Boughton. *Peterson Field Guide: Ferns.* New York: Houghton Mifflin, 1984.

Dodman, Nicholas. *The Dog Who Loved Too Much.* New York: Bantam Books, 1996.

Heinrich, Bernd. "Winter Guests." *Natural History* 110, no. 1 (February 2001): 36.

Hoshizaki, Barbara Jo, and Robin C. Moran. *The Fern Grower's Manual.* Portland, OR: Timber Press, 2001.

Innes, Clive, and Charles Glass. *The Illustrated Encyclopedia of Cacti.* New York: Knickerbocker Press, 1997.

Lange, Willem. "Tales from the Edge of the Woods." *Yankee* 62, no. 1 (January 1998): 94.

Lorenz, Konrad. *Man Meets Dog.* Baltimore: Penguin Books, 1971.

Mace, Tony, and Suzanne Mace. *Cactus and Succulents.* San Diego: Lauren Glen Publishing, 1998.

Milne, Lorus, and Margery Milne. *The Audubon Society Field Guide to North American Insects and Spiders.* New York: Alfred A. Knopf, 1980.

Monks of New Skete. *The Art of Raising a Puppy.* New York: Little Brown and Company, 1991.

Pugnetti, Gino. *Guide to Dogs.* New York: Simon & Schuster, 1980.

Stewart, Doug. "Luck Be a Ladybug." *National Wildlife* 2 (June–July 1994): 30.

Stith, Mark G. "Dabbling with the Daubers." *Southern Living* 32, no. 8 (August 1997): 50.

White, Richard. *Field Guide to the Beetles of North America.* Boston: Houghton Mifflin, 1983.